The Poised Pen

All Things Considered

Published by Poised Pen 2016

Cover design by Robert Edge

Contact Poised Pen: contactus@thepoisedpen.co.uk

Contents

Preface

It is seven years since Poised Pen's first anthology, *Words from Nowhere* was published with work by ten members and a title partially nicked from the shop below where we met. Among other anthologies since *Words from Nowhere* we have been *Out of our Minds* in 2010 and *Half Baked* in 2014. The titles reflect where our stories live and the venues in which we read, our current venue being the Fly in the Loaf pub in Liverpool, hence *Half Baked*. It's a tricky business coming up with a title everyone is happy with, Tony & Friends was almost unanimously rejected and after many, many suggestions it turned out that the title was staring us in the face. All things had been considered.

All Things Considered has sixteen different diverse authors all with their own style spanning fiction, poetry, script and for the first time song.

In loving memory of our creative culture, we're away with the fairies perhaps to be sanctioned. We may have an unexpected perhaps unsaveable long face but everything will be ok. We are on the cusp of the umbilicus, swimming with dolphins, listening to the pitter-patter from the old school on top of the hill. We are an endangered species under the lowering sun, disarmed.

But we all have our minds, that and a poised pen.

So from everyone involved in the Poised Pen writers group we hope you enjoy the latest instalment of our scribblings.

Robert Edge

Catherine Connolly

What I write

Words - one after another - until their worlds form fully; breathing. They speak for themselves, when I listen carefully for them. They work upon their listener, when I send them out into the world – word worlds fully formed – a silent dialogue. Their sentient sentences cast speculative shadows where they spread; my carefully tended phantasmagorical creations and creatures. Form and format, they shape themselves simply, complex, stylistically, such as they will – or as thought wills it.
Experimental
They
Exist.
Existing
They
Are.
We live together, my words and I. My words with my readers.
We are a universe, fantastically formed.

In Loving Memory

Calder will depart for the afterlife a hero. They have ensured it is so, after his return from the raids to them, scarred, otherwise unscathed. They have no wish for him to revisit, reformed as revenant or draugr, to torment them, though Astrid has volunteered to wield the sword to remove his head if necessary. Brenna favours a stake through the corpse if the eventuality arises. They observe the requirements carefully, conscious of their need for perfection. The body is placed into a temporary grave, covered, whilst they sew, creating the clothes to accompany him on his journey. Brenna sings, strong and true, as they sit, imbibing the drinks proffered to her by Selby, one after another. They will help her see her way when the time comes. "Farið vel og með góðum tíma," Selby says, with each. Brenna nods, accepting the liquor filling the bowl to the brim, fingers touching Selby's briefly, as the vessel passes back and forth again. There is no guard for this, their private ceremony. They are family now.

With a glance between them, they raise Brenna aloft, moving her towards the door frame, to lift her on their palms, once, twice, thrice. Now, she sees out and beyond, into the other realms. They lower her carefully, to stand on her own feet. She is ready and they are one in their task.

The women walk together to the water's edge where the narrow longship waits for them, pre-weighted with Calder's battleworn weapons and armour, sail hoisted aloft. The dragon at its head points seaward, pre-seeking the eventual destination from which there is no return. Brenna climbs aboard carefully, placing cushions onto the wood to create the bed on which Calder's body will rest. She accepts no helping hand as she clambers in and then out.

"Far-wanderer – there is the line of my people, where the brave may live forever," Brenna says, standing at a slight distance from the bronze prow. They all nod, before clutching hold of one another closely, then breaking apart, standing together this last time. Slowly, Brenna removes the bracelets on her wrists, transferring them into Selby's outstretched hands. She removes the finger rings enclosing three of her fingers; places them into Astrid's palm. Once done, she turns from the assembled women, walking towards the vessel where Calder lies waiting for her to join him.

Brenna sits beside Calder's cushioned body as his remaining relatives take their flame-lit torches from the villagers who have joined them. She makes no sound as they set them to the oak and drive the boat out into the water. Burning arrows mark their progress as the ship sets sail in earnest. Brenna takes her secrets with her as she performs her final service for her family. Though Calder sets sail for Valhalla, she will chart their true course. Calder departs, presumed hero. She must ensure he faces his gods armed only with the truth. They will decide where he ends up.

The Descent

The ruby red, rounded shape was there waiting, first thing in the morning; strategically set on top of the sheets, when she woke. Truthfully speaking, she has been expecting it for days, having dreamt of the grove of trees from which the junction of the rivers stems and the thick roots topped by the white funnel shaped blooms, amidst the swarms of squeaking shadows.

It is his way of playing, though as far as she is concerned, things are properly played out by this point in time. She needs no outsized reminder of his enforced obligations.

"Hellfire!" she says, before the corners of her mouth twitch slightly at the words. "And damnation indeed," she adds, to an empty room. She splits the fruit in a swift downward motion, causing a dribble of juice to stain the covers. The seeds are packed in tightly amidst the flesh, so she has to dig a little with her nails to pull them out, right from the centre. She counts a sparse translucent six; no more, no less.

"Figures," she says, toying with a pip between her fingers, before raising it aloft and swallowing it down. She shudders as she does so, frowning slightly. "Pigging pomegranates! Still sour, then."

She pushes one after another after another passed her lips in quick succession, once she has stilled herself from swallowing the first. Red stains her fingers, which she licks clean, wiping the sticky residue against her dark dress, irrespective of whether it shows or not against the dark fabric. Their bitterness leaves its aftertaste on her lips, as the seeds churn in her stomach, refusing to settle fully. She knows of old when and where the sensation will cease.

Sephy sits, waiting for her escort into darkness; possibly Darkness himself, though she is most used to the company of obol-eyed Charon on her lengthy descents. Easier to send someone who can't answer back to challenge, query or quandary, she suspects. She has never been trusted to walk the sections of the realm alone on entry, though left to her own devices on leaving.

"Take me to my husband," she mutters beneath her breath, rolling her eyes. He tends to keep her waiting, despite the early fruity wake up call.

She feels them already – the simple skeletons, the frozen, the eternally blood-spattered alike. Soon she will – must- pass amongst them again. It is small consolation that she must serve only three months. They do not – cannot – care, though for a time they are her people, without being capable of answering as such.

The door in front of Sephy opens and her eyes acknowledge the figure crossing the threshold. She crosses to him, holding out her hand to take his. They clasp palms and the bony fingers close firmly around her own. Sephy nods.

"Ready," she says. "Again." The journey into the heart of Hades is long, capable of seeming to encompass one's lifetime, though Sephy knows the truth. She will endure this cycle forever on repeat.

Mermaid Cove

We cannot rest
Whilst water surrounds us,
Submerged, we sing;
A game, of sorts,

Once won,
We keep our catches
Closely,
'Til surface seduction
Calls out
Again.

By Dark

By dark
They lure
Sleepers unaware
Into disaster;
Pillows bereft,
Leaving warm dents
Where bodies lay -
No more.

Eventual

If I lay here,
Would my world
Become a universe
Eventual,
Invisible,
Of
Possible histories,
Infinite in
Potential,
Beyond me?

Imagination's Citadel

In the quiet hours,
Imagination's Citadel
Can be seen clearly,
By those who know
Where to look,
Using their
Focused
Mind's eye.

For Now Or Forever

The boat is already waiting, close to the bank, with the water lapping, as Cara approaches the edge. As she puts a foot on board it sways slightly as her weight disturbs its easy equilibrium. The rope tethering the vessel swings in accompaniment.

"Fare, please," a thin voice demands. Cara looks down, seeing the tiny hand outstretched towards her. She frowns slightly, squinting.

"What are you?" she murmurs, looking into the bleached face with its dark pupil-less eyes beneath wispy strands of white hair; looking through the skin itself, where objects behind it display themselves.

The girl shrugs her shoulders. "Ferrymaid, for now. Fare taker forever, perhaps, if day due Danakes remain unpaid - with lesser lads 'n wenches."

"I..." Cara says.

"Pay up or hop off," the girl interjects. "Others'll be waiting. 'Tis not my matter when women wish to wander. Though we'd call it wasteful when we're all wanting 'n wishing for farther in..."

"We?" Cara asks.

The young girl shakes her head quickly. "What may be – as well as what was once, though but half-formed; what should be, should circumstance allow."

"Large thoughts for one so little," Cara says, brow creased. "Do you know what they mean?"

"Do you?" the girl retorts. "Since my fare's still owing? Will we journey - or will you bide by the Styx? Your choice; where others have little hope of it." After a pause, "You must be dead, you know. By definition. I'd be dead too by now, if I could."

"Would you?" Cara asks, shortly followed by, "Sorry? What?"

"You'll understand, in a while. 'Tis not for me to say."

"Isn't it, though?" Cara asks. "Is there no choice in anything for the Never Weres? Or is that Never Ares? Do you yourselves distinguish between the two? If not – shouldn't you?" She lets out a quick breath.

"Remembering now, a little?" the girl queries. "Though your Isle awaits. You'll be better there," she adds. "Forget about this; me. You'll mean to remember. You'll even try to – but won't."

"Will so!" Cara exclaims. "God - you've got me regressing!"

"Not possible; not now," the girl says. "Time's passed and ebbing."

Reelistic Crimes

"Seen this?" you read, as Mal's message pops up on screen, paper clip towards the bottom. Double clicking, you pull it up – video playing full colour, minus sound.

"Jesus!" you exclaim, seconds in. "You sick…" you start texting, before another message intercedes.

"Got it from Tone. Tells me it's some comp. Interactive. Been doing the rounds online. Big buzz on Twitter. Collect the clues - catch the killer – all that jazz."

Eyes narrowing, you examine the clip again. The quality is sketchy; pixilation grainy. Likely shot on a hand held. "Figures. Found footage," you mutter, rolling your eyes, before concentrating on the image. The blonde's eyes are wide, as she cries for the camera; the ligature tight about her neck, held in surgically gloved hands. The angle shifts momentarily, giving a glimpse of script across one wall, before returning to the girl. "Cryptic Clue One," you say, watching closely. "Guessing people are on that already." On-screen the girl struggles wildly with her mask-clad assailant, as the cord tightens around her neck. Involuntarily, your eyes shift from the action, as the man – or what you would guess to be a man from both height and *his?* build – induces air hunger and unconsciousness. A final glance and you shudder at the abandoned body, prostrate on the floor; livid marks circling her throat. The clock counter reads close to thirty seconds; no longer, as everything fades to black. "Pretty damn realistic," you murmur, grimacing. "Sure better be staged."

"You game?" Mal is asking almost immediately. "Money's good for the winners. Might be worth a punt."

"Prefer Reverend Green with the rope myself," you say, straight off.

"Nutter," Mal replies. "Suit yourself. Means more loot to sweeten the pot. Signed up for updates already. Some sort of feed for subscribers."

"Best of British," you send back. "Rather you than me. Seriously. Bit close to the bone – or should that be wire?" you question. Mal doesn't bother answering.

"How goes it?" you text a couple of days after. A message appears on screen seconds later. "Reelistic Crimes," you read, frowning at the title. Your heart starts pounding as the image appears and begins to play.

Of The Moment

The sun is high and Hel can feel it on her skin as the beat reverberates from the sound stage. She sways a little with the rhythm, bottle in hand, feeling the moment up against her skin.

"Hey," a male voice says.

"Not interested," she replies, without looking. "Try the beer tent. You'll score there, for sure."

"Cheers," the voice replies more warmly. "Literally, I guess."

"Figuratively, too," Hel responds, turning towards the man. "I guess." She shrugs, before the corners of her mouth quirk, surveying the dishevelled dark hair and lighter eyes as she looks upward. "Hardcore tat," she appraises. "Corruption, though? Really?" She shakes her head, letting out a breath. "Classy." Her eyes roll, as her shoulder shifts away.

"Where exactly did you think a guy like me would hang out?" he asks, raising an eyebrow. "Kind of perfect, if you think about it. Pretty great rate of success, courtesy of lowered inhibitions.."

"I'm sure," Hel says, laughing openly now. "Like I said - beer tent's where you want to be. Best of British - though you won't need it, several ales in."

"Spoken like a true observer," the dark haired male says.

Hel shrugs. "Doesn't take much."

"You haven't asked me what I'm doing here."

"Besides hitting on the wrong women?" Hel asks, tone sharp. "I *have* already told you."

"Besides that," he agrees, voice remaining level. "For what it's worth."

"Is it?" Hel asks. "'Cos you can't take a hint, can you? It's not like I haven't been clear. I mean - really - is it?"

"Well, I *am* Corruption, as we've already established," the man says, an apologetic note entering his voice. "Seeing as you were enjoying the moment, so to speak, I couldn't resist stopping to chat.."

"We're done now," Hel says, blunt. "You're leaving."

"Hedonism," he replies. "Took me a minute or so to put a name to the face. Got it now though. New one on me. Takes a careful eye - though once you know what you're looking for…"

"Jesus!" Hel curses, looking around hastily.

"Long gone," Corruption responds. "New Guard all the way, sweetheart. Get with the programme." He smiles. "Y'with me yet?"

The Crescent Quarters

They will take you to the Crescent Quarters on dark, moonless nights, if you know where to find them. That is Test One. Do you see them yet? Those shadow silhouettes with painted faces, casting themselves as chameleon; as tricks of the light? They are there to locate, once you know how; in the hidden spaces. Once spotted, they show themselves immediately to the sharp eyed. Such is the bargain they made, though no one knows with who or how it was arrived at. The details remain shrouded; lost in time's passing. Perhaps they too will be rediscovered, though not today, not by you. They are not your task. You are already upon it.

Will you take them by the hand, to let them lead you where they will? That is Test Two, though none can say whether yes or no means pass or fail. All stay silent on that score. The decision is yours alone for the making. You have taken it already.

The way lies above ground, through the Long Ages; that you gather, as the white gloved hand leads on and into the dark. You fancy their cries beat upon you, as the long, carved staff hits the ground; it's constant click the audible companion to your own footsteps. Your guide keeps his counsel, face forwards, dark eyes averted. What do you hear? What calls to you? Is it the jolt towards justice? The sound of sympathy? What do you feel stir beneath your bones? Is it the burn of revenge? That is Test Three. Multiple choice. You have your answer ready.

The top hat bobs beside you, leading you further in. Deeper; still deeper. The shaded city is side to side now, its buildings all around you; its shadows upon you. You hear them now, around you. The souls stirring to meet you. They hear you breathe; feel your heat amidst their chill.

Your heart jolts as you realise it is you and them now. Your guide has stolen silent from the scene, somehow; somewhere. Now you have no choice. You must find your own way back or remain amongst them. It is your final test.

Wifely Wisdom

All Hallows Eve was the night Will lost his head. Literally. Fortunately, his wife had some insight, being versed in witchcraft, as she was.

"Not to worry, darling," she said, as the body crawled over the threshold, "though you might want to wait there for a minute whilst we work something out – the blood's staining the floors and I don't want to have to worry about castings on top of this one. We need the energies."

The stump assented, as far as Cara could tell. At least, it was dipping and swaying the right way.

"D'we know where and when you lost it?" she asked. "A point in the general direction would save time in the searching, that's all." Will's finger hit the air aimlessly. "I'll take that as no," Cara surmised. "Guess that's not so surprising, considering."

Cara sighed. "You know we'll have to work quickly, given we don't know where to look yet?" Her husband's neck waggled at her. "No need to get tetchy!" Cara exclaimed. "I'm not the one who got careless with my bodily bits on my travels. Plus, I'm doing my best here, under pressure I might add!" The stump subsided in its movements.

"Better. Now, we need a substitute 'til we find the real one. I know just the thing. Have it here. Lucky it's still intact. Hadn't gotten around to carving it." Cara moved towards the stove, placing both hands on the rounded orange object on the work surface. "Might be a bit heavy," she said, doubtfully. "We'll have to see. Bend down, there's a dear." Will's body obliged, stumbling to kneeling. "There we go!"

Cara thought for a moment, whilst the newly assembled body remained motionless. "Nose and eyes," she said, decisively. "This might sting," she warned, as she inserted the knife's point into the pumpkin's surface. "Stay still." Will did, as she carved. "Mouth will have to wait," she said, after. "I can only do so much magic at once and shedloads went into animating the head. You can wait 'til tomorrow, sweetheart, can't you?"

There was a pause before Will's body moved violently. "That's a yes, then," Cara responded, placid.

Civilisation's Pillars

Some say civilisation's pillars are submerged beneath the surface, depthless deep devastated, if you dive down, their particulars preserved in red rock and crumbling concentric canals, pure white ivory at the heart. Alien ancients of no place are held captive by the ocean's sway; an isle overthrown, swallowed whole in silt slavery, their shattered city-soul secreted sunken beneath the host gulfs and eddies of a boundless continent. Thus did decline and chaotic corruption bring their just ends full circle in chastisement within one day and one night in the first fight. Now, year on year and with the turn of the tide the sea's triumphant swell drowns out the ghosted warning whispers of the geographical fiction seeking to break their water bonds and rise towards liberation's lights.

They dwell there still in rumoured existence under muddy subsidence, a semi-forgotten nation. One day they may make themselves heard by civilisation, so some say. They hope not to be doomed to failure.

Lord and His Lady

Lord lives – seventh of seven times seven before him half-hearted. His Lady took his thumping whole, instantaneous, while he held still willing. Now, the Eve the Year Dies is upon him, a multitude of little deaths gone before; blood sucked from its protective layers around his bones by his lady's lips. He holds no regret. The hollow it should reside in has no beating inhabitant.

Lady was hearty, laughing whilst life sustained her, duly bound, its beating within her fist. Lord is her promise to herself, self-gifted – though their contract was written between marrow margins long ago, had he but known it. Some things are as she wills it. She is tired now; tithe falling due. All things must end. Men though – mortal - live in the moment. Licking her mouth, Lady summons her Lord to his final standing.

Lord's skin was sold at birth, time ticking afterwards. He answers at All Hallows, son for father, as did son from father before him. Half a heart for a future functions well enough. Thus, Earl, eloquent, escaped his lover's arms without compunction, to answer to another's call. Time, irresistible, reaped its tithe on him. Lord still lingers.

Lady savours sucking Lord's soul from its moorings; his life having no need for it, once wholly consumed. Lord ponders their partnership, deceased, eyes downcast. Head raising, he turns away from her. He gave love freely. Bad bargaining cannot catch hold, where its central sacrifice is missing, though she has had his heart from him. Time take him, too, instead. All things must end.

Grandmother's Strings

Bidziil wants to tell Spider Grandmother before it is too late. The strings bound in – out – across his lips prevent him, as he quails. They are taut on his numb lips. He imagines they bleed, though there is a gap where the truth should be. The missing minutes – *hours?* – gape black in his memory when he seeks them. With them they have taken the daylight, leaving only pitch in place.

"What you say?" Grandmother demands, waving gossamer attached at her fingertips before him. Bidziil gazes at the wizened woman, helpless. The threads – criss cross – across his lips prevent his answer.

"No matter," she says, as his tears fall. "Talking God told. His winds whispered well. You wind into my weaving or I boil your bones, yes?" She pauses, considering. "Your choice. You speak?" she asks, sharply.

Bidziil watches, wide-eyed – webbing straining across his mouth; hands tied to the tree forks splayed right and left behind him.

"Bad child!" Grandmother says, frowning. Creases form deeply on her brow. "I teach you to heed before your bleaching! Then you join my collection, no? Your bones shine on Spider Rock." Thin fingers clutch Bidziil's own, though he cannot feel it as the bindings are snipped from his hands by claw-like nails. He stumbles to his knees.

"Up!" Grandmother demands. "You work or you boil. Yes?"

Bidziil nods fervently; his mouth remaining bound.

"Perhaps I cut other strings if you behave," the woman says, eyes hard. "You prove not a bad boy first. You see?"

Bidziil nods again.

"We weave with shadow," Grandmother says. "Quick now! 'Til fingers bleed!" She holds her hand towards him – thread floating with the movement. Bidziil grasps it clumsily.

"We wind together – yes?" Grandmother says. "I show. You watch.

Close now!" The woman laces web with dew from the tree's branches, where it glistens in the moonlight. Throwing it high, it catches – pinpricks forming amidst the black. Bidziil watches, eyes raised.

"See? Stars, yes? We make our Glittering World, nightly. You try now," she bids.

Bidziil casts his thread skyward – seeing patterns created; concentrating. He only glimpses the long bones by his feet from the corner of his eye.

Hannah Coyle

What I write

I write about faeries and magicians, about the worlds hidden behind our own. Everything I write has a touch of magic and a touch of darkness because there's nothing quite so fascinating to me as the damned. I write about deeply flawed, irredeemable characters and troubled characters and occasionally, good characters. I write about things that blur the lines between likeable and dislikeable. I write about myself, little pieces of me in every character, from something as small as a preference to as big as a personality trait. I write the edges of the box. In short. I write stuff.

Away With The Faeries

Never trust the faeries. It was what everyone was taught growing up. Never trust the faeries, never make a deal and if you see them, look away. Perhaps that was why no one thought to call on them when we were attacked, though it was within our rights to do so. Never trust the faeries and never make a deal because what they ask for is always steeper than what you can give. I can't think of many things steeper than death.

The path I'm on is dark, too dark, with only the suggestion of trees outlined by the moon. I glance back, nervous all of a sudden because I've been alone for too long and surely someone's noticed. The raiders didn't take many captives and even they can't make a mistake when counting up to five. Captive. I was a captive because I didn't think to make a deal, as would be my right because there's no steeper price than a faery price, except I can think of some.

There's movement behind me - a familiar shout. Five captives were taken, three girls and two boys. This girl is called Riley, my neighbour and friend of more than nineteen years. I wait for her, because it's only polite.

"Rowan!" She stops before me, hands on knees as she breathes so she must've run quite a way. "I thought - I thought I'd find you here, best place to get yourself lost, ey? Those mercs were going crazy when they realised you'd escaped, I- I managed to get away in the confusion."

It sounds believable. I look into the dark behind her. She's caught enough breath to walk now and so we walk.

"Where's your sister?"

"Ah." She purses her lips. "She's… still with them. I couldn't get her out. I'm sorry."

I eye the trees. There's every chance I could escape within them, but there's also every chance I could break an ankle or even my neck and there's also a good chance that Riley could keep pace with me. These are our woods, we know them well.

"So how long till they catch up?"

"Not long. I'm sorry, I'm so sorry." She really does sound sorry. It won't stop her from turning me over for her sister though. I don't blame her, or begrudge her, family ties were all she had left. Even so, our walk is strangely companionable. I watch the trees. Never trust the faeries.

Never call on them. Never make a deal.

I can hear footsteps now, the shouts of men. Not long at all. I take a breath. People died because they wouldn't take the risk, because the lessons had been taught too well. Still, everyone knew the words.

"I call upon the faeries, for I wish to make a deal."

The words echo. Riley looks strangely horrified, as if I've betrayed her, and I suppose if everything works out then I will have. She opens her mouth.

"I'd like to order a book."

We're in a library. Riley is standing before a desk, behind which is a disgruntled man clearly not at peace with his role as librarian. Likely he is a displaced professor now relegated to desk duty. Riley is endeavouring not to notice his displeased nature. She's probably missing the cute boy who'd managed this library for the past few years. Except we've never been to a library, or at least not this one. I don't recognise it, not the desk, not the shelves beside me going up into eternity.

"There's no ceiling," I observe. The librarian frowns at me. Riley looks concerned. The ceiling's back. I wonder why I'd thought otherwise. I try to remember why I'd been looking for something different, why I'd thought I should be elsewhere. I study the shelves, the books all in neat rows of colour, each title an illegible tangle of words, as if I were in a dream. About halfway up there are ornaments, except they're perched so precariously that they should've fallen. A dream was right. In dreams the impossible looks possible - it's only when you realise what you're looking at cannot be right that you wake up. This time I didn't shout my observation. Instead I closed my eyes and remembered.

"What do you want?" I whisper, and when I open my eyes I'm in a wood. My wood. I can see Riley - he's on the path, surrounded by the men who'd stolen us. They're all looking for me, casting about as if I've disappeared, which is exactly what I've done. Something slips and I see behind what's happening. There's a golden world beneath our own, ever changing and never still and looking like every fairytale land rolled together, and there's a boy, looking like every impossible prince though he's not. "What do you want?"

The faery smiles. They don't smile like us, I realise, there's something entirely different behind his expression.

"For you to stay with me," he says, "for all eternity."

He unfolds his fingers and holds his hand out. Never trust a faery - they cannot lie - but that does not mean they tell the truth. Behind and beyond him I can see my old life. To accept the hand is to accept eternity in a gilded cage, to refuse is to take a handful of years in an iron one. I realise, at last, that my people did not die for fear of these creatures, they died for fear of never dying. The naïve grasp for immortality but the wise recognise it for the curse it is.

"Rowan!" Riley shouts, looking at me but not seeing me.

I take the faery's hand, not because I don't fear immortality, and not because I fear Riley and the men. I take it because I fear reality, and there is nothing real in Faeryland.

Bren Curry

What I write

I write words, lots of words, then I delete them; then I write some more. This has been my pastime for almost fifty years. Sometimes I finish writing and it becomes a short story or poem, but what I really desire is to write a novel.

I have thirteen lever arch files of unfinished novels, and am currently writing the fourteenth. The majority of the novels are magical realism and mostly aimed at the young adult reader.

I believe in faeries, ghosts, dragons, spirit and other things people can't see; I believe one day I will finish writing a novel.

Looking for Lucas

I stood by the window looking out into the garden. The rain oozed through a gap in the wooden frame and trickled down to the sill.

A small hand crept into my left hand. It felt cold and clammy: or was it sticky? The fingers curled into my palm and around my thumb trustingly. It stayed there tucked into mine. I closed my hand over it automatically. It seemed to me that many years had passed since I held my child's hand, although it had only been two years since the accident.

We just stood there.

Very still.

For a long while. Still.

For longer than I wanted, longer than I intended, I stayed silent.

I didn't want him to vanish. I didn't want to break this spell of mother and son holding hands once again.

I could have wept, but I didn't.

Instead, I whispered. I kept my voice low in an attempt to draw out this precious moment. The angels had brought him to me as I had asked them to; and here he was.

He was here beside me.

I was holding my son’s hand.

He was close to me once more. My boy, who could never keep still for long, who found all of life fun, until that fateful day, just stood beside me.

Still.

Wordless.

My chattering noisy son said nothing, but as I slowly looked down on his golden curly locks and pale skin, he looked up at me with eyes so filled with love that it was all I could do, not to cry out.

I spoke so softly that he could have mistaken it for the fall of a leaf or the wisp of a breeze, but he understood.

I knew he understood.

A mother's instinct? The strong bond of a mother and son? He listened as I spoke.

'I love you, Lucas.'

A slight nod. His eyes fastened on my face.

'I will always love you, Lucas.'

Again that slight nod and a barely perceptible tightening of his fingers around my thumb.
'You were just a two year old when they took you from me. Do you understand?'
He blinked. I knew he understood.
A shout pierced the moment. I looked up, Lucas looked away.
I could feel his hand slipping from mine. I couldn't show emotion. I wanted to hold this blond-haired boy of mine once more. I couldn't cuddle him, of course.
'Will you come again tomorrow?'
The space in my hand that had once been filled with his was now painfully empty.
'I would like to see you again. I will wait for you here, in this very spot. Will you come?'
My child nodded and was gone.
I had suppressed my emotion and the maternal feelings he had stirred, whilst he was standing by my side. Holding my hand. I couldn't risk sending him away for ever. I had to tread carefully so as not to push him away.
I whispered again to the wind.
'I will wait for you.'

I waited again in the studio.
I waited from first light, trying not to think of the possible scenarios that would prevent him from coming.
I stood looking out of the window. The garden around the studio was overgrown. It had once been neat. Fairy ornaments had danced around the flowers and path. Around the door I had tacked fairy lights, and Lucas thought it magical.
There was a strong smell of honeysuckle. It had taken hold of the outside of the studio and run rampant, wrapping itself around the walls and roof. Entrails of it squeezed through all the gaps in the wooden walls and what was left of the roof and spilled over on to the floor.
The light trespassed through the grubby window and fell onto the toy garage I had been making for Lucas that day. It stood there covered in muck, dust and webs like some unloved, derelict, inner city petrol station.

I'd been standing at the window in the studio. Lucas was with me playing on his trike. In and out of the studio.
In and out.
In and out.
There was a storm brewing. I called him in out of the rain. I saw a flash then heard a loud crack, and all of a sudden the roof caved in.
I screamed.
Den, our neighbour, came rushing over. He saw me holding on to Lucas. Holding on to my son, my dear son.
It was too late.
They pulled him away from me.

The sky was quickly becoming grey. It was going to rain. The light was fading fast, and the clouds had gathered in an angry blanket overhead.
I feared he would not come.
I waited longer than I intended, never taking my eyes off the window.
He isn't coming, I told myself. But as I stood there his hand slipped into mine, and I squeezed it gently.
There it was again. That look of love. Those trusting eyes gazed at my face.
I smiled at him.
'I will always love you Lucas. I will always be your mummy.'
'Love you, Mummy.'
I could have wept.
'Lucas, Lucas! There you are. What are you doing out here?'
I reached out to my mother, but she didn't see. She walked straight through me, to sweep up Lucas into her arms.
'Mummy.'
'No, Lucas darling. Mummy's gone. Mummy's joined the angels.' I saw the tears in her eyes. 'Come with Nanny. We'll bake some cookies.'
I watched as they walked down the garden path.
Lucas turned and held up his little hand in a wave.
I waved back and blew him a kiss.
His tiny lips made a 'mwah', then he turned back to my mother and snuggled into her neck as they went into the house.
I knew he wouldn't visit me at the studio again. The next time he sees me

he will be old with children and grandchildren of his own.
I felt a presence behind me and heard the rustle of opening wings.
'Are you ready?'
'Yes.'
I was enveloped in brilliant light.
'Bye, Lucas.'

Defying the odds

Aries: Stay indoors today. Today you will get a visit from the past. To avoid a nasty surprise, don't leave your house.

'What a load of tosh.' Marina folded up the newspaper and threw it on the coffee table. Draining her mug of coffee and inhaling the last of her cigarette, she grabbed her handbag and rummaged through it, looking for her car keys.

Not in her bag.

Marina made a habit of leaving her car keys in her bag. She had a last look, emptying out the contents on the coffee tale.

They still weren't there.

'Damn those blasted keys.'

She snorted and looked out of the window. The sky was heavy and grey. The wind made a long low whistle through the trees at the corner of the house.

She grabbed her coat.

Something jangled in the pocket and, relieved, she thrust her hand into the gap.

Just her house keys.

Reluctant to leave the warmth of the house, she opened the front door and stood there weighing up her need for cigarettes against the chances of being caught in a downpour.

She needed her cigarettes.

Curling her hand around the house keys, she made her decision and stepped out onto the path, closing the door behind her. Despite the heavy, threatening sky and the strong wind that was tugging and pulling at her and forcing its way into her coat slowing her progress along the pavement, it wasn't as cold as she first thought.

Marina pushed her hood down onto her shoulders. Once her head was uncovered, the many hands and fingers of the wind began attacking her hair. The hair slide was wrenched from her crown and hair tumbled down the front and sides of her face. She grabbed a handful from in front of her eyes and pushed it behind her ears, only to have it snatched back and wrapped around her face like a veil. Again she pushed it aside, and seeing the zebra crossing stepped into the road.

As the wind whipped Marina's hair out of her grasp and into the air, a small speeding white van turned the corner narrowly missing her, but slammed straight into the side of a black cab spinning it around and clipping it into the side of Marina's hip and thigh, before both vehicles came to a halt on the opposite side of the road.

For a while she swayed, but managed to stay upright.

A car horn, loud and insistent, was ringing in her ears. Feeling dazed, she surveyed the scene in front of her.

The black cab and the small white van were entwined like a Yin and Yang symbol. Marina could see only the drivers. Thankfully there were no passengers in the black cab.

The drivers were arguing.

They were standing in the road, oblivious to Marina, concerned only about their vehicles and their livelihood. Arms waving, fists shaking, practically forehead-to-forehead tension, anger and frustration.

They didn't notice her.

'Are you hurt? Do you need help?'

Marina turned. She grabbed hold of the concerned young man and wouldn't let go. Her face an unhealthy pale grey, was rapidly turning paler.

She saw him hesitate. He looked as if he didn't want to get involved. He glanced over at the drivers still arguing, then at the mangled vehicles and finally at Marina, who had started shaking.

He reached for his phone and dialed 999. He then told Marina, 'What does it matter if I arrive at the hospital later than I intended? Dad is in a coma. He won't notice what time I arrive.'

Marina kept her hold on the young man. The police arrived seconds before the ambulance, and while the paramedics were attending to Marina, the police began to take statements from the drivers. One of the policemen couldn't take his eyes off Marina; he kept looking over his shoulder and staring at her.

The policeman unnerved her.

She tightened her grip on the young man.

'Come with me,' she pleaded with him. 'You are going to the hospital anyway – you may as well have a lift there.'

Marina was ushered into the ambulance.

The police approached the young man. He told them, 'This junction is an accident hotspot. My father had his accident here. He was a pedestrian and on his way to see his new granddaughter, my daughter, at the hospital. He sustained head injuries.' The man swept his hand around to emphasise the area. The road narrowed very quickly after being a wide junction. 'There should be traffic lights rather than a zebra crossing.' The young man’s temper increased. 'My father is in a coma, linked up to a machine that breathes for him. We may have to make the decision to turn off his life support. This road is a death trap.'

The police asked questions.

After giving evidence to the police, he clambered aboard the ambulance to sit next to Marina. She turned to thank him but stopped abruptly when her eyes locked with those of the policeman staring at her through the gap in the closing doors.

Unease crept though her.

Someone had left a newspaper behind. It was the same one she had read that morning. Marina opened it at the coffee morning page to re-read her horoscope. Her eyes scanned the columns for Aries, but to her surprise there was no short warning at all, it was just a rambling general account, very similar to all the other signs. She threw the newspaper to the floor, shrank back into the pillow and sat in silence until the ambulance stopped and the doors opened again outside the hospital A&E.

'It doesn't feel broken, probably just bruised.' The doctor turned to wash his hands in the small sink in the corner of the cubicle.

Marina sat looking blankly at the wall in front of her. The young man had left her as soon as the paramedics helped her into a wheelchair. He'd muttered his get well wishes then made his exit towards the wards in the main hospital.

The doctor huddled in the corner with the nurse on duty and after a few minutes of whispers and nodding heads, he approached Marina.

'To be certain, I am requesting an X-ray, although I am sure there are no broken bones. I would normally send you home after a routine check, but because of the shock of the impact, and to err on the safe side, we will keep you in overnight for observation.'

Marina showed no reaction.

The doctor glanced at the nurse who shrugged and pulled a face. He turned back to stand in front of Marina and bent his knees until his face was level with hers. He had a kindly face. 'I am off duty after this shift. I will sign you over to the care of my colleague. Sister Belling will arrange for you to be taken on to ward one, and the night duty doctor will see you tonight, then again tomorrow morning. No doubt you will be discharged after a good night's sleep.'

Marina's hands were shaking. She hadn't had a cigarette since she'd left the house that morning. She felt tired, sick and dazed. There was a tight knot in the pit of her stomach and her throat felt constricted. Something in the way that the policeman had stared at her worried her. They hadn't interviewed her at the scene, instead she heard them tell the paramedic they knew where she lived and would catch up with her later. What did they mean by later? Why did they know where she lived, or did they mean they expected to find her in the hospital?

She wanted to move, but her lifeless legs were pinned to the bed by an invisible force and her shoulders felt leaden and too heavy to lift off the bed.

She shivered.

At the nurses station they were discussing Marina. They had seen previous cases of people shaking as much as Marina was. After an intense debate, they telephoned the doctor on duty for advice.

Minutes later, a nurse was dispatched to the pharmacy, returning with a mild sedative. They took Marina's blood pressure and pulse then handed her a glass of water with the tablet.

The doctor visiting her was vaguely familiar. Marina struggled to wake up. Her eyes were heavy and her vision hazy. She tried to ask if she could go home, but her words fell from her lips in a molten heap, each running into the other, making no sense, so she gave up.

Rahas, the doctor, bent over her and shone a small torch in her eyes, lifting her eyelids up one at a time to do so. He was so close to her face that she could feel his breath on her skin.

The breath was icy.

Marina's pulse quickened, her skin paled, beads of sweat collected on her forehead, her whole body became clammy, and fear crept slowly and painfully up from her feet. She made to speak again but although her lips moved, no sound escaped. The doctor moved closer until he became a blur in front of Marina's eyes. His icy lips brushed her ear and he lowered his voice. 'You shouldn't be in here. You threw away your chance. You had been warned.' He moved away, leaving Marina chilled.

The evening crept into the night. Marina alternated between waves of fear-induced nausea and drug-induced sleep. She tossed and thrashed about, suffocating with night terrors. They started as the regular bad dreams she experienced at home, when the doctor, whom she soon realised was the protagonist in her original bad dreams, was holding her close and breathing poisonous gas into her mouth. At one point she awoke from the depths of a nightmare, only to find herself being pulled back down in to it, the doctor grasping her again by the neck and clamping his mouth over hers.

She gasped for air.

At the bottom of her bed, the nurse was talking in hushed tones to the doctor. Marina drifted in and out of consciousness. She wanted to listen to what they were saying but the effort of concentrating made her feel nauseous and drained her of energy. She was drowsy. It was easier for her to give in to sleep than fight it.

Marina opened her eyes.

The nurse and doctor had disappeared. Walking towards her was the young man she clung to in the road. He stopped at her bed.

'I'm on my way to visit my dad and thought I'd look in on you. I asked at A&E how you were and they said they'd kept you in.' Marina didn't reply. He shuffled awkwardly on the spot. He had his baby with him. 'I've brought my daughter in for my dad, though of course, I know he can’t see her, but I hope he will sense her.'

The young man moved closer to Marina, holding out the baby. The baby cried out loud and didn't stop screaming until she was moved away from Marina. Feeling flustered, the man made his excuses and left. The baby calmed down...

Marina made no sound.

She had neither acknowledged the young man nor noticed the baby. She felt sick. Every time she awoke she felt worse. Her limbs ached and burned from the sensation of thousands of hot needles pricking her skin.

When Marina next awoke she had a tube in her arm. Her eyes wouldn't open enough to see properly, but she could just about make out the shape of a drip stand and bag. She felt a frisson of unease. Marina sensed rather than noticed the police enter the ward. They were accompanied by a nurse.

Marina slipped into sleep.

'What's wrong with her?' One of the policemen bent down and peered into Marina's face.

'Shock, mainly,' replied the nurse, 'although she is a bit of a puzzle. We can't find any other reason for her rapid withdrawal. She wasn't seriously hurt in the accident. Just bruised.'

'It was almost on the spot where she had her car incident months before...' One of the policemen, the one who had stared at Marina, suddenly announced where he had seen her previously.

The sergeant glanced at him and raised his eyebrows.

'She caused an accident by driving her car erratically and at speed. I'd swear she'd been drinking, sergeant, but she tested negative for alcohol. She pleaded that her foot had slipped off the brake on to the accelerator when a cat had run out in front of her car, sending her careering out of control.'

'What has that to do with her being the victim in this incident?'

'Nothing really, I suppose I find it strange... As if I'm missing something. Like a piece of jigsaw that doesn't fit, but should.' He stared at Marina.

The sergeant then turned to the nurse and gave instructions to be notified when Marina was feeling able to communicate. They left, but as they went, Marina managed to open an eye, only to catch the policeman staring back at her. He made a slight motion of running his finger across his throat, although his facial expression didn't change.

The shaking started again.

Three nurses ran to her bedside and busied themselves, checking her drip, blood pressure, temperature and pulse. Marina was sweating, but her body was clammy and cold. Her skin had a greyish translucent pallor and her eyes appeared too small in her sockets. The nurses held a hushed discussion at the foot of her bed, glancing over occasionally at Marina.

The doctor was called.

He stood by her bed. A figure in black, dark hair, dark beard, black clothes. Marina tried to open her eyes wider but the fluorescent light shining behind his head blinded her already sensitive and sore eyes, so she closed them again.

As the doctor moved closer, her body tensed. The shaking became jerking convulsions and the sweat ran from her brow. He held his hand out to the nurse and she filled a syringe from a phial and handed it to him. He leant over Marina and whispered in her ear. 'You'd been taking drugs and the police missed that, didn't they? You went straight to your car after doing cocaine and drove straight into the pedestrian.' His breath icy against her ear sent her into more convulsions as fear gripped her heart and throat. 'The innocent gentleman you mowed down is going to have his life support switched off tomorrow. The police may have missed the evidence but we didn't. You can't run, no one can, your sins will always find you out.'

He injected the sedative.

Hallucinations plagued her day and the night terrors increased. Marina fought to wake, but a group of hooded figures dressed in black, dark facial hair covering their features, pulled her back into the horrors of her subconscious. In the darkest area of the pit she was surrounded by floating black semi-transparent birds or devilish creatures, at first swooping down at her then circling her at speed snapping at her face and brushing past her. In her nightmare she ran towards a gap. In her bed she was thrashing about, grasping and grappling with the bed covers as the faceless beings chased and grazed her.

She managed to open her eyes.

She was really awake.

For the first time in two days she could see clearly the beds, the curtains, other patients asleep, and at the top of the ward she could see the nurses station. She opened her mouth to shout for help. As she did so a black figure appeared from behind the bed frame and clamping his mouth over hers, breathed in. Marina was pinned to the bed, unable to move, unable to breathe, and the figure continued to suck in the air from her lungs. Clamped onto her lips until it was satisfied it had sucked her last breath, the figure then evaporated into the air and disappeared.

Marina lay there lifeless.

Sounds from an alarm startled the young man. He heard a gasp. He looked down at his daughter who had ceased her cries and was gurgling happily. Realising that something else was different, he turned to see his father lying in the bed with his eyes open and smiling at his new granddaughter.

In his office, Dr Rahas Khama checked his list of patients for the day. He crossed off one and marked a tick against the other. He placed his notes and the files in his case, cleared his desk and left the office, locking the door behind him.

His job was done.

A Creative Culture

A Villanelle

A changing work of art on the skyline, when you're leaving
Along a street called Hope, two Cathedrals to call our own.
If I can't create in Liverpool, why am I breathing?

On a bench, a bronze of Eleanor Rigby sits dreaming
Life moves on, new talent, fresh breath, creates alongside old.
A changing work of art on the skyline, when you're leaving.

Two football teams, red and blue, keep thousands believing,
Sing, you're in my heart and soul, and you'll never walk alone,
If I can't create in Liverpool, why am I breathing?

Pioneers, Hornby, Ellis, Hughes, Ross and more, did the leading,
Willie Russell, and Alan Bleasedale, make theatres our own.
A changing work of art on the skyline, when you're leaving.

Humour, Lambananas, a vibrant, city heart beating.
Ken Dodd and Bessie Braddock share a joke 'neath Lime Street's dome,
If I can't create in Liverpool, why am I breathing?

We have old life to tell the tales, new life to stop it grieving,
Talented Waterhouse, actors, Baker, Catterall all home grown
A changing work of art on the skyline, when you are leaving
If I can't create in Liverpool, why am I breathing.

Ashes to ashes

As he waited in the doorway of the old warehouse, he remembered a conversation he'd had with his uncle, one night, as a young child. He could picture it vividly.

'Why does the moon remind you of the Bone Man Uncle Frank?

Frank, face hidden from the moonlight, had cast a faint shadow on the bedroom wall.

'They slipped into Liverpool on small ships, steered by the light of the moon. The human cargo had endured rough and stormy seas, many were left weakened by the journey. Promised a better life. As they disembarked the Bone Man lined them up in the moonlight, segregated the healthy from the weak. The weak were unpaid, worked to death. Cheap labour. The healthy were herded to a warehouse at the dock.'

Frank made a slashing motion, with his hand on his neck.

'He sold their organs for research, stored their bones in trunks; that was how he was discovered. The sculpture outside your house is in memory of the dead.'

James still felt the nausea rise in his stomach, even though he'd later discovered that the sculpture, 'A Case History', was nothing to do with the Bone Man.

The story was real though, and it had started again.

In the police he was put on the team investigating the trafficking, disappearances, murders, mutilations, every clue led to a dead end. For years it had given him sleepless nights, then came a lightbulb moment, sparked by something his wife had said after vacuuming their hall.

He knew he should mention his suspicions to another officer, but if he was wrong...

He saw the lights go out, waited ten minutes to make sure the building would be empty, before breaking a window to get in.

He was about to vomit into his handkerchief, when Frank found him snooping in his workshop.

Frank made ash from bones.

'Why Frank?'

'Ash is saleable, it has so many uses. No point trying to hide the bones.'

He picked up a carving knife and lunged at his nephew.

James still had the smell of burning in his nostrils as he stepped into their hall, closing the front door behind him. He brushed down his jacket, and checked the carpet for ash, it wouldn't do for his wife to notice it when she vacuumed this time.

The Flibbity-Jibbit

She entered the ballroom floor, with a smile
Looking around to make sure we were watching.
Waits for the music, head held high,
Toe pointed, then she started her dancing.

She whirled and swirled,
Bounced and flounced.
That flibbity-jibbit.

With Nell Gwyn neckline, tattoo on her shoulder,
Her gypsy style dress moved as she swayed.
Her partners, agile men who were older.
Each tune, another dance to the audience she played.

She whirled and swirled,
Bounced and flounced
That flibbity-jibbit

Kept up the pace for three hours, on a packed floor,
Bosom heaving, bottom rounded and fleshy.
She entertained, knew all the dances and more,
Agile, light on her feet, rippling and swishy.

She whirled and swirled,
Bounced and flounced
That flibbity-jibbit

Through the old time she romptied and pomptied,
Straight backed, stately, knees up but jolly.
Through Latin, arms expressive, she shimmied,
Head turning, legs long, steps quickly and slowly.

She whirled and swirled,
Bounced and flounced
That flibbity-jibbit

In Jive, high kicks, moving and rocking she titillates,
Jiggled and swiveled, shook her boobs to the song.
Teasing in tango, with sexy moves she scintillates,
Foxtrot was smooth, seamless turning, gliding along.

She whirled and swirled
Bounced and flounced
That flibbity-jibbit

Then when the organ disappeared in the ground
She applauded and beamed at the crowd,
Skipped from the floor, cheeky wave all around,
She picked up her crutches, then hobbled off out.
That flibbity-jibbit.

Plumber's Mate

My drains were smelling in the heat of summer
So phoned ' Drain O'block' to send out a plumber.
I recognised the back of his bum on the floor
He turned, I knew straight away I'd met him before.
We chatted as he worked, but I can't pretend
I was bowled over, when he cleared my u bend.
Though I knew we had something worth pursuing,
And while I watched him set about gluing
The joints, I asked him for a date, saw him blush,
He accepted so quickly, I felt a hot flush.

We make an odd couple, he's short and I'm lanky
He wipes his nose on his sleeve, I use a hanky
I hail from West Lancs, he's Scouse as they come.
I look like Olive Oil, he looks like Tom Thumb.
I talk far too much, he's quiet 'cause he stutters,
At the end of the day, really none of that matters.
We got on fine. You can't describe him as hot,
But I'm desperate, and single and like him a lot.
He is scruffy, beer bellied, and barely luke warm,
I'm no model, flat chested, older and worn.

He moved in. Now I always have flushed drains,
A large double water butt for when it rains,
No leaky washers. He fitted a water meter,
I have a new boiler and smart immersion heater.
We don't sizzle or set the bed sheets on fire
Just take my word, it's not all dampened desire.
We have warm snuggly nights, jacuzzi baths,
Beer, wine, pork scratchings, TV, plenty of laughs.

The house is OUR home now, not his or mine
It will do us quite nicely, until the end of our time.
We share the cooking, chores, company and laughter

Together we'll live the dream 'happy ever after'.
As we grow old, I'll always bless that wiffy hot summer,
When I found my soul mate, in my very own plumber.

The Princess and The Dragon

I hear the crunch of slate and gravel, and slowly open one sleepy eye.

My body is tired and it takes me a while to realise that the sound is coming towards me.

I sleep a lot more these days and by the approaching sound of the crunching slate and shuffling gravel, it appears that I have forgotten it is the day of St Ivor, or why else would one of the townsfolk dare to come near my lair?

I must be getting old. Wearily, I lift my head.

Hang on a minute!

Why is it so quiet?

Have I slept through all the reverie and festive binge drinking, the sports with fireworks? Surely not.

I struggle to open my eyes fully, so deep was my sleep. Why won't they stop this nonsense? It is 2999; in six months it will be the new millennium.

Making her way towards me is not some luckless girl chosen by the villagers, but the princess Terrwyn herself. There are no villagers watching her progress up the mountain and I am not surprised, because it is not yet sunrise. I know now it is not St Ivor's day.

She walks with her shoulders slumped, most unlike her. I hold Princess Terrwyn in high regard; she has more fire in her belly than the Diffyn-gwr (Kings Guard) and is braver than all of her father's court, so seeing her walk without her usual aura of proud spirit puzzles me.

I wait until she is within range, then send her a warning flame.

She stirs from her thoughts and stands straight-backed, legs slightly apart but firm.

Ah, her spirit is awake.

Her body language shouts stubborn.

'You don't frighten me.'

'I don't?'

'No. I have watched you for years.'

Then we have both watched each other. This could be interesting.

'And what did you see?' I didn't mean to spit, but as I spoke I showered her with sparks.

She stays in her same position, back straight, trousered legs firm and attitude defiant. No, she definitely isn't afraid of me, she doesn't even flinch.

'I saw a way to a better life.'

She's smart too. I play along.

'What did you see?'

'I saw a way out of our town. I saw a chance to escape the suitors my father chooses for me. I saw freedom.'

'Yes?'

There is a pause.

'You are the key to my freedom.'

'And how do you suppose I become that key?'

I raise myself up to my full height and in doing so I spy a figure running clumsily in our direction.

Terrwyn spins around to see what has attracted my attention.

'I don't believe it!' She turns to me. 'See! See what I have to put up with. My father will have sent him. I can't move in this awful town without someone telling my father.' This time she moves her foot, only

to stamp it down hard on the slate, sending splinters into the air. 'Oh. I might have known; a noble knight.' She spits on the ground.

I like the girl. I like her a lot. The princess has spunk.

'Princess Terrwyn, your father has sent me to save you.'

'You needn't bother! Go back to my father and tell him you were too late.'

There is something about this knight that I do not like. He does not show any fear, he has not even glanced in my direction. I experience a warning rush of fire to the throat and my chest burns. As I listen to them, I take in the knight's appearance.

'Your father the king has decreed that whoever rescues you from the dragon...' He still doesn't so much as glance in my direction, '... shall inherit his kingdom and marry you. So I've come to take you back.'

I can smell rotten vegetables mixed with bad hygiene. A memory awakens inside my head but I can't bring it to the fore.

She points to me. 'This is 2999, you are supposed to be extinct.' She turns back to the knight. 'And as for you, you should get a real job. Do you think I want to be a part of all this stupid nonsense? Grow up!'

I watch the knight arrest a scowl on his face, and twist it into a sneer.

'I like a girl who's masterful. I will do you a deal then, princess: you give me a kiss and I will leave you alone. I won't claim the lands and fortune. I will walk away and let you fight your own battles. How about it?'

The princess laughs. Despite her brave and boyish façade, her laugh is hypnotic, like sweet music cascading over smooth rocks in a stream. I am mesmerised and caught off guard for I have taken my eyes off the knight, and in that careless moment he has already lunged at the princess.

The memory bursts in my head like shards of glass from a smashed bottle. A troll. A fetid recluse from the Snowdon region! My jaw opens to roar; a split second too late. Before she can struggle, he has gripped her and planted his mouth over hers for that kiss.

The world turns into slow motion.

Horrified, I watch as her tanned freckled skin sprouts white hairs and her small frame bends slowly until she is on all fours. Her feet become hoofs and scrape willfully against the stone, her ears point upright, her small tail points down and all the time she is bleating.

The knight is indeed a troll; moss and mould in his tangled hair, ugly lumpy skin, fat nose, jagged teeth and the smell of a ripe cesspit.

Anger burns as a tight ball in the furnace inside me. I pull myself up to my full height as the ball of fire pushes its way up my neck and out through my mouth and nose. The troll picks up Terrwyn and holds her close to his body. I divert my head quickly to avoid burning the princess as well as the troll, and the flames fall to the side of the triumphant troll, who shakes a fist in the air.

'Losing your touch, pyro-boy.'

The troll backs away with his hostage still shielding him from an attack by fire. Smoking mad, I launch my heavy but cumbersome frame in his direction, and by some spectacular gymnastic moves, manage to swing my tail around behind him. Such is the momentum generated from my base and along the length of my tail, that the lash from the whipping it builds up, knocks the lumbering Troll forwards.

He releases her goat form as he falls and she takes her chance to leap off and scramble along the loose chippings, out of his reach.

I hurl a firestorm of large hungry flames, and they rain down on the troll.

He gives a long, loud, piercing cry as he grabs my tail and sinks his teeth into it.

The effect is instant.

The numbness spreads like freezing tendrils from the bite.

My wings open to take flight. I hover over the running fireball and rain down more fire and flame in an avalanche of rapid fire until, suddenly weak, I fall to the ground. The troll hurtles down the mountainside and out of sight.

I have failed.

I should have finished him off; only if the troll dies will the princess be released from the goat's body.

I drag my tail back into my lair and inspect it.

Stone! My tail is turning to stone and soon my body will follow. I can't stop it. It is beyond my capabilities.

The princess trots over to me and licks my tail.

'It's no use.' I shake my head and point to the back of the cave.

'Go through the cave. At the end, on the other side of the mountain, is Blaneau Grogau. The townsfolk there will look after you.'

She steps towards the back of my lair and turns to look at me.

'I'm sorry, Princess.'

She nods and trots off.

The cold freezes my tail and creeps up my back.

I close my eyes.

I awake to the sound of fireworks, and karaoke singing assaults my ears.

Oh for goodness sake. Not again!

Someone, somewhere, is screeching a god-awful rendition of 'I will go on'. I lift a clawed foot to keep out the assault on my ears.

No claws.

No scales.

I look down. No tail!

Standing a few feet away from me is Terrwyn.

'The troll died?'

She nods.

I look down at my ragged clothes and dusty old body. My eyes are drawn to a glistening mark on my shoulder in the shape of a teardrop. It's not true love's kiss but it was good enough to transform me.

'Did you expect a handsome prince?'

She is smiling.

'Sorry to disappoint you.'

She links my arm.

'It's better this way. We can just be friends.' She gives me a playful punch in the ribs. 'I don't want a boyfriend, if you get my drift.' She winks at me.

I am grinning. It is a wide grin showing off centuries-old teeth.

'Suits me. It is the year 2999 after all. I predict there will be big changes in the next millennium. Even in Llemwynw!'

The Turning of Autumn

She watched faeries in their finery, twinkling and dancing in the night sky.
He glimpsed planets, millions of light years away, because science is fact not fancy.
She reached up to draw down the moon, and danced in the moonlight.
He reached up to draw down the blinds, he couldn't sleep in the moonlit room.
She skipped across the lawn between the toadstools and faerie rings.
He moaned that the lawn needed aerating, and raked up all the fungi.
She chased the white unicorns crashing onto the shore, and raced barefoot over the dust of mermaids.
He gave her an account of the amount of pollutants in the oceans, and cursed the sand creeping into his shoes and socks.
She laughed and told him to lighten up.

He scowled and told her to grow up.
She pressed the golden leaves of Autumn, and collected the beads of giants, as an offering for the Mabon Goddess.
He cursed the falling leaves, littering the paths and garden, and scoffed at her creative arrangement of dying leaves and wrinkled conkers.
By the next fall, her breasts, that had once suckled new life, were puckered and decaying, with tumours the size of giants beads.
She saw Angels in the white feathers that floated past the window.
He swore at the moulting pigeons, messing up his patio.
She saw wings, spread out, and hands reaching down to grasp hers and take her peaceful, trusting soul up to theirs.
He saw hands reaching out to shake his, and the box that held her beautiful body, lowered down.
He watched, with misty eyes, the twinkling faeries in the night sky.
He reached to touch her face in the moon, and yearned to see her dancing once more in the moonlight.
He sat amongst the toadstools, and wished on the faerie rings, dug his feet into the dust of mermaids and let the roar of the crashing unicorns, cascading on the shore, drown his howls of anguish.
In the autumn he pressed the golden leaves and putting them on his bedside table, added them to his growing collection of white feathers.

Turn around Toxteth

The short list is out, for this year's Turner Prize.
On it, jaw-dropping news, what a surprise!
A street in Toxteth that was facing demolition
Is among the entries for Turner nomination.

Turn around Turner, the idea's simply a dream
Combination of residents, working as a team.
The owners, some bought their homes for a pound,
Liked the proposal, and thought it dead sound.

Plans were drawn up, designs set in motion,
Houses stripped out for, creation, renovation.
Forget Emin, the only beds seen on this street
Are bushes, flowers, (no weed), all made very neat.

For twenty years it's been empty. A neglected L8.
If Cairns Street wins, well, that would be great.
So Scousers everywhere, please raise your glasses.
Here's to Toxteth; rising like a Phoenix from Ashes.

May the prestigious prize start with a pound house.
And the best Turner entry, turn out to be Scouse.

WAR 1916

When I join my new unit in the Australian field ambulance, division one, it is a huge shock to my young body. The unit is very regimental, more so than my old unit, and I have left my friends, including Billy and Pete, behind. My eighteen-year-old head can't cope with the enormous change without my best friends.

Lonely but not alone, there are 40,000 of us trainees camped along the six or seven-mile stretch of the canal from Tel-el-Kebir, but miles away from home, and separated from my family and friends, I feel miles away from home, and separated from my family and friends, I feel isolated and homesick.

A great tiredness sweeps over my body where previously hope and light-hearted camaraderie had lodged. I drag my legs, my shoulders are weighed down, and the nausea for home in the pit of my stomach threatens to force its way into the open every waking hour.

I am about to lie down when the door bursts open.

'We have orders to occupy the reserve trenches against the Bedouin along the canal.'

I gasp.

I am not the only one to be alarmed but my mouth is too dry to ask questions.

'Isn't that a bit too close to the action, sir?'

I give Joey a look of gratitude. Thank goodness some of us were able to speak.

'No lad, it's not close to the front line. You won't need your mum. It's quite safe.' Some of the lads laugh and Joey looks mortified. With a camp full of testosterone, it doesn't do to show a weakness in emotion or strength.

I run my tongue along my lips but it is barely moist enough to make any difference.

I long for Toowoomba, for my friends Billy, Pete, Ned and Jack. I yearn to be kissing Doris after the dances.

What am I doing here? Crouching in dirty holes in the ground, sleeping in overcrowded camps with strangers, miles from family and loved ones. For what? For a country on the other side of the world that I have never seen.

I only joined up because I wanted to be a doctor. We thought it would be a lark, a bit of a laugh.

Well, I'm not laughing now.

The homesickness is getting worse. I try to carry on and be brave. I can't appear weak in front of my new unit. After two grueling route marches of five and seven miles, I start with a fever. I suspect that, at some point, my homesickness has disappeared and instead become an illness. I am convinced that I have mumps.

By the time the fever starts, I have become accustomed to my compatriots in my unit, and don't want to let them down. We are being sent to France and I don't want to miss out or leave them a man short. I can't tell anyone about the mumps.

For the next few days, we make route marches of seven, ten and twelve miles. I am exhausted and at times burn up with the fever. I weaken considerably and am sure that I become so bad it is noticeable. Nobody mentions it and I haven't become close enough to any of the men to confide in them.

The crunch comes when we are forced to route march to Tel-el-Kebir battlefields; this was where Viscount Worsley defeated the Turks in 1882 after his occupation of Egypt. Unknown to me the mumps have slipped down to my groin. My temperature is high and I struggle to complete the march. The sun beats down and the pain gnaws at my head and burns the back of my eyes. The sweat from heat and fever runs down my face, but still I carry on.

I collapse after the parade, and am carried to the hospital on a stretcher where I am examined by the doctor. He confirms my suspicion that I have mumps but I also have the added complication of paratyphoid with a temperature of 103 degrees and rising.

Despite the nursing staff, with the help of the doctors, bathing me night and day with cold baths, my temperature swings from 105 to 103 and back again. For two days, I lie at death's door, dipping in and out of this life and the next. At one point, I awake to hear a doctor say he would be surprised if I made it through the night.

I fill with anger.

I'm going to let mumps defeat me. No man was thought a hero dying from mumps. If I join my unit going to France, even in my weakened state I could still fight. If I lose my life in active service my family could hold their heads up at home. I have to get out of the hospital.

My break comes when I have a visit from my two friends. I hear a familiar voice.

'Charlie, how are you,matey?'

I open my eyes.

'Bill. Can you get me out of here?'

'You'll leave here soon enough.'

'I need to ...'

'Can you walk?'

I try to walk but am too weak, and my legs just crumple under me.

Bill rubs his chin and mutters something to Pete who nods.

Next thing I know, they have borrowed a stretcher and smuggle me out of the hospital. How on earth they manage to get me past the nurses at the bottom of the ward and through the camp, but they do.

We board the train under cover of darkness and leave Tel-el-Kebir after midnight. I have a bad time in the open wagon. I can't get warm and have to fight from being pulled into a dark abyss. Once or twice I catch Bill and

Pete exchanging looks and nods. I presume they think me foolish and probably a burden to my unit, but my pride will not let me give up. Again it occurs to me that it is unusual that nobody has stopped us boarding the train.

After an uncomfortable night, we arrive at Alexandria. With Bill on one side and Pete on the other, practically holding me up, we march to the wharf to board the Kingstonian which is to take us to France.

Escorted by two cruisers, we move out of Alexandria harbour. I hear orders being given to collect our life belts and wear them all day and sleep with them under our heads at night.

Bill is reluctant to take me down to the deck, again he exchanges glances with Pete.

'For goodness sake, Bill. What's with all the secret nods and looks? I'll be fine by the time we get to France. Now let’s get those safety belts.'

Officers are calling out the names off a roll call, and handing each man who answered a life belt. I hear Ned's name being called and try to attract his attention, but he ignores me. Hurt by his lack of acknowledgement, I turn back to Bill and Pete. They shuffle their feet awkwardly but say nothing.

I wait.

My name isn't called.

I carry on waiting. The officer doesn't even look up at me, and starts to put away his notes.

I realise he is going to walk off without an explanation.

'Oi, Sir!'

No response.

It dawns on me then that Bill and Pete haven't been given a lifebelt either. Neither of them seem bothered that their names haven't been called out.

‘What’s going on?’

They don't answer. Bill turns away, and Pete sticks his hands in his pockets and looks down. I repeat my question. Bill is the first to speak.

‘Didn’t you think it odd when we appeared by your bedside?’

‘Odd? You are my friends. Why should it be odd that you came to see me?’

‘Mate…’ Bill doesn't finish. The officer appears on deck and is walking towards us. Bill and Pete stand together, each holding a hand up to me in farewell, and fade from my vision.

I hardly hear the officer, so astonished am I at their disappearance.

'What are you doing out here? Where is your belt?'

'My friends…'

'What friends? Your name!'

I give my name and this time it is the officer's turn to be surprised. He checks the list from his pocket for my details.

My name has been crossed off as 'invalided out'.

I ask about Bill and Pete. Their names have never been on the list. I try to remember a detail, but fail.

I am ordered to see the doctor.

It is days later when I sadly work out the appearance of Bill and Pete, but, incredible as it seems, it was thanks to them I was where I wanted to be.

Robert Edge

What I write

I did not find Poetry, Poetry found me.

When I started my degree in English with Creative Writing I naively hadn't considered I would be expected nor did I want to write poetry. Meeting my first year tutor James Byrne combined with some considerable personal turmoil at the time meant I discovered a passion for poetry. I now find I spend more time writing verse than fiction. I am currently working on a project with a landscape photographer combining his images with my words as well as creating a versified tour guide based on visits to museums and art galleries.

Lunch

Strength fails at sub-zero temperatures, a contrast to the superhuman grip around my wrist. He exits through the thick door, delightful smells drift momentarily inside then the door slams shut with an airtight thud. Silence and darkness coexist; only cold and pain keep me company. Lunchtime's over and I know I'll be lucky to see a face before four.

I must have drifted off, as I wake he hauls me onto a table; I grab him with my remaining hand. A waiter's voice;

'Cheeks and liver pate.'

We always joked about the name when we ate at Lector's.

R.I.P. Len Wood

Len had one of the more dangerous professions of the eighties. Though famous for throwing caution to the wind, Len unlike many of his contemporaries had a health and safety record second to none. Many of his friends, Big Ron, Black Beauty and Ken from Dorset lost careers and some their lives through not wearing the right safety equipment. Len had a long career for which he was famed and whether it was through a well developed immune system or just good timing on withdrawal, the real tragedy was his early death choking, as he did, on a nostalgic seventies muff.

The Assassination of Jane Eyre

For want of betterment I took upon myself, dear reader, to find game employment in the education of one such as myself, but five or so years prior. My willingness, nay my desire, to impart knowledge unto such a young woman whilst scarcely being an adult myself did, I do declare fill my heart with trepidation not felt hence. Surely there is no nobler employment than to want a student to outperform their tutor. Twas dear reader, all to come to nought as the crosshairs of that most deplorable man Winchester, with a loud bang, did end my days prematurely.

The Boy Wonder

At five years old:

The definition of
Euphoria
noun [mass noun]

December 25th: Christmas morning
The light-headed heart fluttering feeling when opening the living room door to find an abundance of presents distributed over the floor, on tables, chairs or any other hard surface.

If there is a better definition of the word it has never been found. The Scalextric has been lovingly assembled to spare both impatience and desperation. The telescope is out of its box, mounted on a tripod and pointing out of the widow at a dark cloudless five a.m. sky. Not to be eclipsed, a pair of powerful binoculars hangs on their strap, set for days of adventure to come. Cellophane sealed posters, Cadburys selection packs and a shiny silver torch with buttons that change the colour of the beam. A new pair of trainers with three stripes, not four! A Doctor Who scarf expertly knitted (clearly not by a ham-fisted mother) and a sonic screwdriver to replace the pen, which has had to make do in absence of the official toy for so long.

As the years roll on the definition of euphoria has evolved into a shadow of its former self. By the age of eight the shine has all but gone, dulled somewhat by expectation, somewhat by a loss of, for want of a better word, innocence.

Approaching his tenth year the boy is slipping towards:

Cynical
adjective

Christmas morning.
Seen it all before there are no surprises

Expected to exchange gifts of a commensurate value (not enough pocket money)

At this point perhaps a pertinent gift would be a dictionary but this boy needs something much more significant though perhaps less tangible.

Teetering on the brink and fuelled by hope and playground gossip, he both wants to believe and does not want to be thought a fool for believing in Father Christmas. A new phrase is born: Fears for Peers

Mum and Dad were braced for a Christmas of overspends and tantrum management when to their surprise, just before Christmas and a week shy of his eleventh birthday the Christmas list read:

Dear Father Christmas,
I have been a really good boy this year and I know I asked for loads of stuff at the garden centre but I really only want one thing and I promised Mum and Dad that it wouldn't be too expensive so please, please, please can I have a sense of Wonder?
Thank you
Chris x

Wonder
noun
[mass noun]

A feeling of amazement and admiration, caused by something beautiful, remarkable, or unfamiliar: *On waking he viewed with the wonder of a child the gifts he had received.*

21st Century Beveraging

Of all the invented jobs created to fulfil a sense of worth, perhaps the title Barista is the most grandiose. In case you've been living in a cave for the last ten years, it describes a person who serves in a coffee bar, a place which of late has exploded in popularity. In an entirely unscientific assessment it's probably true to say that weekend clientele can be divided into roughly four quarters.

Firstly, there's the lone male who wishes to escape from home for whatever reasons, deliberately ambiguous the lone male clearly has a subtext to which we can only infer a meaning. He may have just murdered his wife, chopped off her arms and her legs, stuffed her in a suitcase in the loft and popped out to read the paper with a full fat latte. On the other hand he may feel depressed, on this, Valentine's Day and want to be amongst people to alleviate his crushing fear of dying alone.

Secondly, there's the loved up couple, usually young excessively well groomed and a polar opposite to the lone male, they inadvertently exacerbate his feeling of discomfort and loneliness. They barely break eye contact usually only when glancing at their unnaturally luminescent beverage to stir the crushed ice within. Had this been another day the likelihood would be no eye contact and time spent mostly updating their virtual friends on what a lovely time they are sharing with their significant other. Shortly prior to leaving they would take the obligatory selfie to add to their status before exiting the coffee shop only to be replaced by clones of themselves.

Thirdly, children! We were all children once and in a bitter twist fueled by vanity, jealousy and nostalgia I would choose to exclude children from such pursuits as drinking in a coffee shop. Their invasion of the public house is now absolute and it would appear nowhere is safe from these immature halfwitted shortarses and their digital world. Disposable income which used to be known as pocket money has reached embarrassing levels as the purchased whipped cream chocolate infused meals in a glass testify. The calorific value must be at least the RDA for an average adult and if we are not careful it won't be long before these establishments need to widen their doorways.

Finally, there is the single parent, split almost 50/50 men and women.

The women generally carry their younger offspring whilst fathers are more likely to be a man with a pram. Foolishly they believe that coffee shops are a rung up on Ronald's or the Colonel's establishments. Replacing as it does the well-publicised high fat low nutrition meals with a high sugar low nutritional drink. Their children dressed like miniature adults with shrunk in the wash sensibilities, insincere hugs and neck scarves worn regardless of the weather.

This is the rough cut and, as such, there are a number of different categories which make up a minority of the coffee dwellers. The old dears or, as I like to call them, *the tubigrip army* come to look at other people's children. They show off the fact that they too have a Facebook account which they access expertly with their iPad, other tablets are available, though the brand makes them oblivious to their existence. Like the lone male and the theatrically affectionate couple, this serves to alienate the children from their once all-consuming pastime of the big blue 'F'. Nothing says old hat more than an old woman in an old hat. In an attempt to become more continental and cultured we have, in fact become the antithesis of the notion: Americanised.

You as the reader may get a sense of my cynicism and general contempt for popular culture and you'd be right. Like the barista I have developed a grand title for my own line of work. Aimed at the people who may feel a little embarrassed at the ease with which they slot into society, they want an edginess; a distance from the accepted, generally to not feel like a sheep.

Surely my pioneering work in the field of cynicism puts me amongst the greats such as Lacan and Freud, Saussure and Barthes. In years to come the Cynacist movement will have the traction of the feminists, structuralists, psychoanalysts and all the other 'ists' you can think of.

Afterbirth

D-Day
Shoulder barged twisted dangerous breech
Eight pounds of screaming bloodied meat
The third and the final, no more, no more
Oh Christ not another boy!

Christmas excites like nothing else
The boy's wonder
The joy that is
A child's anticipation
Is, in adults disappointment

Dad's Dad's dead
Oblivious to oblivion
Hard plastic bricks my inanimate friends
Burgundy jumpers are knitted by hand
DEATH TO CELERY

My hairy best friend has two extra legs
My other has too but she purrs when she's happy
Amiable friendship though shortlived they're pleased
Goodbye to your whiskers and fur wrapped cancer
Goodbye to your wretched disease

Education is hard
Playing fool is much easier
To smile in a dunce's hat
Hindsight wins typically, as always
And it's they who are laughing now

Dead-end job, pride for working class dad
Rose tinted specs for a blue-eyed boy
Ill-fitting career defused not enthused
As a drama unfolds on stage
The gelatin-silvered vignette

Goodbye to the dog boisterous confidant
Goodbye to your judgeless ear
Goodbye to another dear, dear friend
Our loss is the world's loss to bear
Goodbye to Dad so remarkably unremarkable

Hello to a wife I never thought likely
Hello to a sweet child of mine
Then goodbye to mother the child won't remember
And to feelings
Just feelings, goodbye.

Bread Van

Bread van, pop man
Coffee walnut whips
Thirteen and a half pence coke
Daily mirrored chips
When wireless meant a radio
When diesel fuel's for trucks
Lamborghini posters
Libraries full of books
Benny Hill the Ronnie's too
Morecambe's word to wise
Michael Bentine's Potty Time
Jim fixed it with his lies
Public information films
Charlie says and green cross code
Clunk click everyone
you fools Savile's on the road
Party four, Watney's red
The pubs shut after ten
Love/hate tattoos on hand

Platform soles for men
Bolan M & Bowie D
Androgyny on tap
Showaddy Waddy, Boney M
Quality v crap
Street parties, Russell Harty
God save the Queen
Sex pistols Jethro Tull
And all that's in between
Working class shattered glass
Disaffect youths
Thatcher's rise to prominence
On a tide of plastic truths

Long Face

Resplendent
in highlighter pen yellow
in cerise
in turquoise
with spots
or with stripes
Bunched in a cage
with a hard hat
So many hopes
so many
ride on a long face
Why the long face?
tragedy
She falls at the third
It's ok though!
Little man's fine
Though we can't say the same for long face

She can stand
But she cannot run
No matter
all is not lost
She'll earn a Michelin star
For her new master
On go the others
Oblivious
to potential
Oblivious to oblivion
Still you dropped two sizes
And that dress is Devine
The hat is sublime
When you walk home
The blisters will keep you company
You can mop up the piss
From your legs with
Your spare knickers
You keep in the Primark clutch
That two hundred quid dress
now a bib for the champagne breakfast's encore
'But I only bet once a year'
Indefensible mantra
Lacking in foundation
And off the hoof.
Tell that to long face.

Beautiful Blue

My beautiful blue
Stubborn unflinching confidence
Hides a well worn insecurity
Eyes of a child spy
The world of
alien concepts
Of adults who please as they do
and do as they please
To those they lay
with contemptuously
Condemnation of blamelessness
as the facts hide the truth
of a ship sailed without direction
Of the money for old rope
to a Spanish Armada
Cut free without freedom
to drown in self pity
Where the sirens mock
As only sirens can
Where the demons within
ride a tide of lonely thoughts
of ropes and sharp blades
and paracetamol
To awake with a smile
To the sight of a photo
My beautiful blue
On the bedroom wall
In brevity hides pain
Which returns for an encore
As the sun rises
Through my window.

Remember, Remember the 8th of September

Not that I'm counting
But ten years today
A little old lady on drugs
Slipped away

She had a big problem
In her head, don't you know
A fucking big tumour
decided to grow

This dirty big Tumour
The size of a plum
Resided inside of
The head of my mum

It spread from her lungs
Due to Regal king size
A lottery gift
Where death was the prize

She lay in the side room
I hoped she'd awake
I longed to just hear her
For my sanity's sake

Whispering soft words
Whilst stroking her hand
While the tumour just pressed
Her pituitary gland

The last time I saw her
All grey in her coffin
That big wooden box that
They carried her off in.

I knew that she'd gone
That I never would hear her
Complain of her ailments
Well none of this seemed fair

I wish I could see you
If just for a while
you'd laugh at this poem
With one last wrinkled smile

So ta-rar to me Ma
And to all our good times
We cried, laughed and loved
As partners in crime

Stone cold empathy

She stole a life to make another to adore for her fans
Fake plastic friends confident as fuel for ill conception
She blames
She does not love: She deceives, lies buzz like flies
A broken tooth to a hobnail boot, she blames

Green-eyed monster for sibling rivalry still grips like a fury
She judges
She pays lip service to a service without lips
And forces to a corner where only the square arse would fit
She does not love

Mother said:

If you've nothing nice to say……

He devours conceit the narcissist disguise a competitive lie
Friendship hollowed as shared ideology dies
He Lies
Perjury, be found in contempt for the indignant
Hope hollowed to void
The cheat's conceit.

Audible tactile sensual visual bare-face-lie
He lies
Flirting without flirtation
Fiction wrapped in invention
Topped off with a bow of deception

The child sides, *whole picture's* in disguise
Unaware as he is
He tries
Distortion bends to opposition
As fingers point not to but from the accused

Dashed expectations of stone cold empathy
She glides
Onward merrily forward to reconcile
A promise broken a promise no more
Action taken loves favours lost.

Tortured mind behind watery eyes
He hides
In this loneliest crowd in his finest disguise

Jan Hughes

What I write

Mainly script, the art of visual storytelling. I invent characters and put them in situations, real or imaginary. Getting them through to an ending is the challenge. Spending time in their shoes, keeping them believable and not letting them stray into implausibility is exhausting. It's tempting to use these made up people to air personal grievances, but if I only wanted to rant I'd write a blog. I want them to live their own lives to be criticised or sympathised with becausc they have connected to an audience. It's not easy being them, if it was they would be dull.

Sanctioned

EXT. PASSAGE – NOVEMBER MORNING, 2010

Savage thorns are growing through a chain link fence, prowling behind it a pack of slavering DOGS are PANTING. The fence is one boundary of a deserted passage. The opposite side is a brick wall with five deep evenly spaced niches. Steady rain is falling in the early gloom.

From the far end the prim and proper JANET SNIPE (43) is strutting into view. Her smart unbuttoned mack FLAPPING in the wind over her dark pencil skirt and business jacket. Her hair is neatly pinned up and she is wearing stylish high heeled leather shoes. Over one shoulder is a huge tote bag. Her other hand is struggling to hold her umbrella steady. Battling against the weather she's keeping a wary eye on the dogs as she passes.

A powerful GUST OF WIND mangles her umbrella and she lets it fall. Turning up her collar she hurries down the path.

INT. BED-SIT - MORNING

Thin curtains are filtering winter morning light into a sparse untidy bed-sit. One corner has kitchen cupboards, a two ring hob, fridge and microwave. In the old grate an ancient gas fire in unlit. A large gilt framed mirror hangs over the mantle piece.

On the single bed dark tangled hair pokes out of a sleeping bag. GROANING, IZZY (20) slender and shivering wriggles free. Putting an old jumper over her t-shirt she steps into once fluffy now bald, King Kong slippers.

EXT. A LOW RISE 60'S OFFICE BUILDING, MORNING

TYRONE (32) a bull necked bruiser is UNLOCKING from inside a glass door marked 'Department of Work and Pensions.'

Janet, strands of wet hair escaping from hairpins is BARGING her way through a mixed bunch of PEOPLE waiting in the rain. He opens the door and Janet enters. He shuts it again to a chorus of MOANS and VERBAL ABUSE.

INT. TOILET – MORNING

Trembling Izzy is rubbing goose bumps off her bare, thighs, watching her breath turn to vapour.

For Robert Tressell

Author 'The Ragged Trousered Philanthropists'

Three times named, three times betrayed.
Your body, publishers and the working man.
You wrote to tell us the truth, we didn't hear,
knew our place, hid our hunger, ducked our shame.

Now we place flowers for your memory, in a city
that champions your cause. Divided we lost
the same battles, too late for standing together
after the conqueror has passed on his way.

We didn't learn the lesson, still grateful for
the little we have. We took our hands off the
next man's shoulder and held them out for
a pittance that kept us in rags.

Blood Relatives

A long time ago Holly lived with her four sisters, all called Ivy. To overcome the confusion caused by their lax parents each Ivy also took on a name that suited her character.

The eldest came to be known as Blade Ivy. She lived her life controlled by unforgiving rules, never allowed herself to over step lines of conformity. At night she folded herself up so thin and tight when Holly woke her she was cut like paper.

Following her was Sinister Ivy. No one had seen her face in decades. Fear and dread gripped Holly when she swept by in her hooded cloak made from freshly skinned bats. Corruption and vanity howled under the shelter of her newly dead wardrobe.

Cat Ivy was vacant to everyone but herself. She poked and rummaged through dirty laundry to publicly expose the unclean. Intricately she threaded gossip through other ears until it was all hung out. For entertainment she watched her victims squirm till they perished naked.

Last in the quartet was Evil Ivy. She refined Blade's narrow mind, copied Sinister's vanity and never missed an opportunity to spread hate. She toted her own jealousy like a weapon. Flashing and vicious, laughing when her tongue bled from the vileness of her words.

The town they grew in had been cleansed of anyone with ambition or desire. Without people the buildings cracked open along streets that had dwindled to ash. Each Ivy lived separately in one of the abandoned ruins, blind to the world gone bad. Holly kept her distance.

Sinister was the first to realise the fortunes of the ugly place were getting worse. From her tower block she saw dust grey plants grow rapidly, tendrils entwine to strangle each other until nothing could thrive. She didn't mention the self-devouring forest to her sisters until the day she stepped through her 32nd story window onto a knurled bough of a tree.

'Move lower,' said Blade.

'Stop lying,' said Cat.

'Who cares,' said Evil.

'I do, I'm not and I won't,' said Sinister.

They were at a morning committee meeting in Blade's semi-detached bungalow. Originally built on a cul-de-sac it was now a blip on a bend on a forgotten road. After next door's roof caved it was only a matter of time before the dislodged bricks fell down, leaving Blade in the desirous position of having a house with an uninterrupted side view.

'I am so hungry,' she said.

'Starving,' said Sinister.

'Why hasn't she brought food?' Evil bellowed.

'I'll find her,' Cat offered.

Thin as a pixie Holly was brought before them. Barefoot she slipped a damp moss tunic over her head. Blade started the interrogation.

'Why are you never here?'

'I am busy,' Holly replied.

'Too busy to harvest?' said Sinister.

'There is nothing to pick.'

'Too lazy more like,' Cat crowed.

'Not good enough,' Evil sneered at the others then back to Holly. 'What happens with your time?'

'I am making a path.'

'I told you.' Sinister was triumphant.

'And why would we need a path?' demanded Blade

'We can't stay here forever.'

The four tutted impatiently.

'Did we leave when the shops closed?'

'When locusts devoured all our crops.'

'When everyone else had gone.'

'Before the bridge collapsed.'

Four sets of folded arms confirmed they were not going anywhere. Holly sighed. They left Blade's and went their separate ways. No one saw Cat fall into a very deep hole.

* * *

The next morning Holly was summoned by Sinister to join her on her window ledge. Leaves erupted every few minutes on the tree, Sinister oooh'd and aaah'd watching Parrots in free flight. Pinching Holly hard she asked about the colourful birds.

'Are those feathers?'

'They're flying, of course they're feathers.'

'In all those colours?'

'And more.'

After descending the 697 stairs, Holly spent what was left of the morning swinging metal through growing tissue. It fell leaking along the short but growing trail.

On her way to scavenge for food she passed a hole and stopped to listen to it swear. Cat's broken nails clawing the rim of the crater were quickly withdrawn when Holly stamped on the fingers.

Tired and dusty she entered an abandoned house and glanced at shoes spilling out of a wardrobe. She had no desire to constrain her feet and left the property with a sack full of canned custard and a revolver.

Her battle against the voracity of nature's revenge was painfully slow. One day she veered off to explore under the ominous living canopy and discovered a new plant. Thousands of white and red petals formed deep bowls to hold their potent elixir. Held aloft on hidden stems Poppies danced in air foul as a goat's bad breath.

It took Holly weeks to complete the dress to Sinister's design. Made from the feathers of hundreds of birds, (their plucked carcasses retained for parrot fricassee) it hugged her voluptuous figure. Reds and greens smooth over her hips. Blues and violets plunged to her shapely bust. Lifting from her shoulders fluffy under down.

'Like a glove,' said Sinister.

'Gloves don't fly,' re-joined Holly.

'You said they would.'

'Did I?'

'I've got their feathers.'

'Have it your own way.'

The bough shuddered as she jumped. Splintered bark poked her from bough to bough. Her plumage got torn off by thorns or stuck to acid sap on giant anthers. Shrieks of pain were ripped from her throat and dragged under the growth. With a splat her bruised body landed in the centre of a sundew, fresh meat for the flesh-devouring weed.

Committee meetings now reduced to a triumvirate. At a loss for whom to blame for their sibling's deaths Blade and Evil blamed Holly.

Blade's nerves were well frayed, to calm them Holly brought her soothing poppy drafts.

'It will deaden the pain,' she said watching the milky fluid disappear into her mouth. Evil accused her of poisoning their sister.

'Let her be, she doesn't need it.'

'She wants it,' insisted Holly.

'If she dies.'

'Her grief will end.'

'And mine will begin.'

'Grief lives in the heart, you won't suffer.'

Evil lunged at Holly sparks in her eyes spitting hate. She chased her all over town, through the school with no knowledge the hospital where death lived. They dodged around frail rust ghosts of cars that shivered in their wake then blew away. Only ever two steps ahead Holly was exhausted when she turned at the start of the excavated path.

'We can be free.'

Evil looked from Holly to the light at the tunnels green end and laughed.

'No. Not you.'

Holly tried to sprint away but Evil grabbed her hair and held her tight. She struggled free and ran for her life. She felt the revolver lighten in her hand as the bullet left, peace shattered before her ears filled with silence.

* * *

In a bright kitchen marmalade gold drops from a spoon onto china. Holly savagely butters toast, scowling at Bob who smiles back.

'They were all there,' she tells him.

'The usual?'

'Yeah, I killed them all, again.'

'Good for you.' Resting his hand on her shoulder as he passes to get milk from the fridge.

Holly wipes spilt dry coffee grains from the worktop into the palm of her hand. She briefly resists the impulse to rest her tongue on the raw grains.

'Gone, swallowed, just like that,' she says.

'Hmm.'

Refolding the paper Bob watches her dip her head and poke her stippled tongue at him.

'They'll leave a bad taste,' he says.

'They always do,' she agreed.

* * *

Holly's composure is intact when she arrives at the restaurant. She knows how good she looks in her dress of good white cotton with bold random patches of black and yellow. Sleeveless, her back exposed by the V cut to her waist. The cool interior is welcome after midday pavement heat.

She scans the dining room. Acres of pale floor, crisp linen falling neatly crimped over the edges of round tables. Glittering sparks leap from silver into her eyes. In the shade of her fingers she sees the four women, chatting, smiling. From this distance she can see flamboyant Brenda the family pillar, stable, steady, and oh so, oh so predictable. She is reprimanding a bra strap for exposure on her freckled plump shoulder.

People look at Sylvia for different reasons. Her curving where it matters body is being shown off in a tailored dress. A declaration, she has no intention of dying poor, her ring-less finger signals her mission to find another man with money is ongoing.

Catherine is a feline wisp in blue silk.

Evelyn is dressed to kill. Combat ready, buckle and buttons shining.

Holly watches them sharing a joke.

Someone touching her elbow breaks the moment; a waiter leads her to her family. Promising to bring a menu he abandons her to them.

'You all look well,' she says, as the residue of smiles fade from their suddenly graceless faces.

Invisibly the waiter hands her a menu. Sylvia tells her they have already ordered.

'Oh, was I late?'

'No.'

'What's good?' she asks, ignoring the list in her hands.

'Omelette,' says Catherine.

The waiter is hovering. She snaps the menu shut.

'Potted shrimp, calves liver.'

'We've ordered dessert, this is my treat,' Brenda says.

'I'll wait thanks.'

Now they look at each other, expectant but not curious. Holly does a double take at the two stripes on Evelyn's khaki sleeve.

'You've been promoted,' she says.

'Is that a problem?' Evelyn shrugs.

'No. Well done, you could have told me.'

'You weren't here.'

Oh God, the sniping was starting already.

'There's email and . . . you know.'

Bowls of clear onion soup are put before Sylvia and Evelyn. Brenda's calamari comes with herby mayonnaise. Catherine's half dozen rocket leaves have seen a bottle of balsamic vinegar. Nothing arrives for Holly.

Shamefaced the waiter installs a late ice bucket, his apology lost in Champagne's first greedy gulp of air and bubbles fizzing in five glasses.

By the time Holly's fork is digging for shrimp under the deep butter blanket, their dishes and plates are being scrapped clean.

'Uhh all that fat,' Catherine says.

Holly smiles indulgently at their disapproval before her lips close over a fork full of yellow and sea salty brown.

'So, so, bad for you,' Brenda adds.

'You will be an obese corpse' Sylvia chuckled.

'No self discipline,' Evelyn says. Words delivered with regimental fervour.

'It's potted shrimp not a grenade.'

Holly closes her eyes; vision will interfere with the pleasure of tasting the spiced shore.

It is too much for Catherine she looks away from the table, mutters, excuses herself and heads for the Ladies. Hallelujah rings in Holly's ears, one down three to go. She grabs the waiter's arm when he comes for her plate.

'What's your best red?'

'We have an exceptional Margaux.'

'Two bottles, thanks.'

Catherine is back, averting her eyes from fillet and rib eye, shaking at the sight of lamb cutlets. She barely smiles at her omelette. Holly's knife cutting the tender flesh of dead calf draws a subtle bloody smear on the plate.

'Look who's over there,' Catherine waves at a man who has seen her too late to hide. 'I really must say hello.' She has won prizes for skipping; it is an unbecoming gait in ankle length silk.

'Are you working?' Brenda asks.'Yes.'

'How many jobs is this?' asks Evelyn.

Holly wants to ask how many guns she has.

'Quality not quantity,' she says instead.

'Lost count more like,' Sylvia adds.

'Never get anywhere chopping and changing,' says Brenda.

Again the wine is delivered late. Silence is observed to make the waiter uncomfortable for the delay. Holly sniffs the wine, raises her eyebrows, swirls and tilts light through the glowing ruby liquid and raises a thumb to the Waiter.

She watches Brenda allow the wine to please her.

'Aah Brenda, 30 years in the same house, 25 in the same job, and here we both are.'

'Not a ring between us.' Sylvia eyes the assembled fingers.

'Once bitten,' says Brenda

'What you've never had you never miss,' adds Evelyn.

Humphing they turn to Holly who remains quietly smiling; the wine is a good choice, it is going down well. Predictable wheels are turning in light heads. Sylvia is weighing her own expensive haute couture self, against Holly's dress.

'What are you so pleased about?' she asks.

'My dress.'

'Still find Oxfam amusing?'

'I was wearing it in Barcelona,' Holly says, now tipsy enough not to let Sylvia's snide remark spoil this memory for her. 'Having coffee in the Picasso Museum.'

'I prefer Las Vegas,' Brenda interrupts.

'A woman on the next table said -'

'Oh God another fantasy?' another attempt to but in.

'It was so hot, the shade in the café held me there, she said I looked like a Picasso.' The remembered moment lights up her face. Her sisters turn away.

Fruit bowls overflow with ripe crimson, pungent cheese swells out of a furry jacket, hot cherry dumpling with cream and ice cream for Brenda. Holly taps tissue thin sugar, smooth cream oozes from crisp copper. Her ears are only half open. She can hear their murmurs, their tittle-tattle, opinions not worth a salt and burnished spite.

The ceiling to floor green marble lavatory walls remind Holly of something comforting she can't place. She dabbles her fingers in cold water held in a deep white bowl.

On their way back to the table Holly doesn't bother to tell Sylvia the hem of her dress is caught in her knickers. Graciously she is accepting the nods and winks of strangers, blissfully unaware her sassy cheeks are peeping out from black satin.

Brenda is choking, she spits out a mouthful of red wine, it turns purple down the front of her dress. Drawing more attention to herself by shouting at the waiter, at the end of his shift and tether, he insists.

'That's a good price for a Margaux.'

'Daylight bloody robbery.'

From the corner of her eye Holly sees Catherine slip away.

Brenda turns too quickly to hand her card over and knocks the heavy bottle off the table. Shrieks fill the air as it shatters on stone tiny lacerating missiles embed in skin.

Faces start to bleed as the dregs of wine trace veins on the marble floor.

Evelyn's moment has come she hits the floor shouting.

'Attack on the floor everybody.'

Under the table she comes face to face with Brenda on her hands and knees. Both grab Sylvia by an ankle, screaming she kicks them away. On all fours Brenda reverses out from under the table. Abruptly Evelyn stands, debris cascades off the overturned table into Sylvia's lap.

'Bloody Idiot,' she spits out jumping to her feet.

'Vain cow,' Evelyn throws back.

Brenda vomits her cherry dumpling back to the world.

Holly calmly surveys the once desirable scene of plenty, now a ruinous site of mayhem. As the waiter passes their eyes meet, he looks at her in despair. Unruffled she smiles at him and slips a folded ten-pound note into his hand.

'I won't be coming again,' she says.

David Irvin

What I write

I can answer in general terms as to what I write, however any expression that goes to the quality of my writing will always remain in the gift of others; welcome even when the well-intentioned, constructive criticism proffered by some misses completely the point I was trying to make.

I write, whatever the form or genre, for me first and others second; selfish perhaps but true. It's my hope, of course, that anyone reading my words will react favourably and with the emotions elicited being those intended; if that happens then what I write works, for me and the reader.

Do you look for me?

Do you look for me at daybreak,
as night steals back your dreams?
Do you look for me at breakfast,
when downing one last tea?

Do you look for me mid-morning,
as your day is in full swing?
Do you look for me at lunchtime,
when churches' Noon bells ring?

Do you look for me in the afternoon,
as your working day slows down?
Do you look for me at teatime,
when together we'd be home?

Do you look for me in the evening,
as we'd chat about our day?
Do you reach for me at bedtime,
when we'd cuddle and you'd hear me say…
"I love you"?
If you do, my love, then remember…
You left me.

His Time

He'd never been what you'd call heavy-set or athletically built, especially compared to his contemporaries and making his way to the shop his footsteps made little impression, as they quietly crunched the newly fallen snow.

Trade was seasonal and he knew there'd be only one or two on duty and few, if any, customers. The answer to the question, 'Why this shop and why right now?' was quite simple; he felt it was *his* time.

Should he be discovered the consequences to his liberty, physical well-being and immediate financial situation were too dire to contemplate, but this was something he had to do, right here, right now.

The moment was imminent. His hand in his pocket; the well-used metal, lying comfy filling his sweating palm, would get the job done. For as long as he could remember people had looked down at him, patronised him; well not anymore! By this one action he would proclaim his worth, his individuality.

Hat down and scarf up he entered the premises then stood still, taking in the scene before moving slowly to the counter and the waiting member of staff. He edged forward, closer, ever closer; he had to be close; his hand had to be steady. It was time! With a smooth, well-practised movement he quickly brought up the unseen fist enclosing the metal and purposefully thrust it forward.

'A large Double Choc Chip, with sprinkles, please.' said the five year-old, as his open palm tendered the exact amount in warm, silver coins.

The Mark

To Sam, a life was no more or no less than a commodity with a price tag. As Sam saw it, one person's desire for the premature ending of another's life was an opportunity to make money. The 'who' or the 'why' were of no concern as long as the up-front fee was deposited into an off-shore bank account. Sam regarded contract killing as an equal opportunities business and ensured that all prospective 'marks' were considered, dispassionately and without prejudice, for an early departure into the afterlife of their choice.

Sitting on a stool at the bar the businessman was a few feet away from a group of animated young men who he guessed were salesmen taking part in some corporate bonding session or initiative test, as all were wearing numbered, scarlet tabards that they obviously believed gave them leave to talk utter nonsense in very loud voices. He noticed the pretty brunette standing the other side of the noisy group as she waited to be served. He smiled and in an animated cliché gestured to her, bringing his hand to his mouth, rocking it back and forth. The woman smiled and nodded and he beckoned for her to join him. The tycoons in waiting fell silent and parted like a jealous Red Sea as they allowed her safe passage through their ranks. Clare and Nathan introduced themselves and spent the next hour or so drinking and making and responding to all the usual bland and hackneyed enquiries as to where the other worked and for how long and whether there a Mr or Mrs on the scene? He said he was a buyer for an internet fashion house and was in town visiting suppliers, that he was divorced and had no children. She told him she worked as a PA to the director of an events management company and had recently split from her fiancé. After several more drinks he proposed that as neither had reason to rush home, perhaps, she would stay for a bite to eat?

Each was attentive and responsive to the other's body language. Eye contact was strong when one leaned forward the other followed, when one made a gesture it was immediately mimicked by the other and when one laughed the other did so too. 'Mirroring', the psychologists called it, a sure sign of bonding. A little after 8.00 pm the couple left the wine bar and, as it was a mild evening, decided to walk to a nearby Italian restaurant in Soho. Nathan dropped into the conversation the fact that Karl Marx had stayed in the same building in Dean Street during the early 1850's, when it was a cheap lodging house, rather than the up-market restaurant that now occupied the site. He asked her what she thought Marx would have made of a capitalist system where everything, including life and death, had a price. Outwardly her only response was, "mm... I wonder?" but inside she smiled.

Clare's real name was Sam, short for Samantha. She was thirty eight years old and had been a killer for hire for almost ten years. During this time the number of those she'd despatched had reached twenty four; 'retiring' Nathan would make it her quarter century.

The British Secret Service had recruited Sam straight from university. Being an Honours graduate with a flair for languages and a keen interest in sports and martial arts made Sam an ideal candidate.

Seven years after joining the Service Sam was on assignment in Prague. Her cover was as part of a government sponsored team developing international trade. In the language of the 'Cold War', which had ended with the fall of The Berlin Wall a decade earlier, Sam was a 'spook', more commonly known as a spy. The Service trained Sam to use her good looks and athletic figure to lure foreign diplomats and industrialists into her bed, in the classic 'honey trap', and while there she would tease from them the information she required. In Prague they tasked her to enquire about research into a polymer that could be made finer than a spider's web but was stronger than high tensile steel several times its thickness; the military implications alone were incalculable. She 'bumped' into the development engineer at a glitzy embassy reception covered by local media and quickly latched onto his arm. After drinks, light banter and more drinks, the engineer was under no illusion he had made his conquest for the evening. Later in his hotel room he had become suspicious and then turned violent towards her. She killed him with the edge of her hand in a single upwards thrust to his throat, crushing his trachea, rendering him silent, unable to breathe and very shortly afterwards, dead. The death was reported in the papers and on TV, including pictures of Sam linking arms with the engineer at the reception. She left the service soon after as she'd become 'known' and as a result unable to continue in such work. Being trained in all aspects of security and well able to take care of herself Sam, had no problem finding jobs in 'personal protection' with some very powerful and not always reputable individuals. From time to time they'd asked her to permanently 'retire' someone, something for which she was well rewarded. Sam had become a paid assassin.

Sam employed many methods to kill. Skilled with small arms, rifles, knives and poisons; she could make a head shot at over a thousand metres. Sam still practiced karate and had attained the rank of 5th Dan Black Belt, which meant that, unarmed; she was about as lethal as it was possible for an individual to be.

Information in the dossier on Nathan was confirmed by what he'd told her in the wine bar. Sam was pleased about there being no kids but had there been any it wasn't about to stop her from killing him. Her plan for Nathan was to use the honey trap, to get him back to his hotel room and then once he'd passed out, with the help of a little supplement to his drink, to inject him with a large enough dose of adrenalin to promote a fatal heart attack. The scene that greeted the room cleaner the following morning would leave it beyond any doubt that he'd died in the throes of a strenuous sex session. By that time the adrenalin, a natural substance, would have been absorbed by his body and would not show up as a cause of death at the routine post mortem. Neither would there be reason for the medical examiner to look for the needle mark between Nathan's toes. He would have died as a result of too much drink and too much wild sex. That was the plan and so far everything was going to plan.

The meal was superb and Leonidas Quo Vadis lived up to its well-deserved reputation. As they walked from the restaurant Nathan joked that, "after a meal like that a person could die happy". He was silent for a moment before saying what both had expected would be said but not knowing by whom, "Do you have to go? I don't want you to go. I want to spend the night with you. I want to wake up with you in my arms." There was a pause before she reached up and placed her palms on either cheek bringing his face to hers for the kiss they both knew had been inevitable.

Nathan was staying in a busy, better than average commercial hotel. Sam asked Nathan for his room number, saying that it was better that they were not seen together, joking that she had her reputation to consider. She knew that a well-dressed woman walking confidently through reception and on to the lifts wouldn't raise any suspicions with the staff and she wanted no obvious connection being made between her and Nathan, once his body was discovered.

Sam waited outside the hotel for a few minutes before entering and without any hesitation crossed the reception area to the lifts. Alighting at the sixth floor she made her way to room 601 and knocked lightly on the door.

Once inside she fell into Nathan's embrace and they kissed over and over again. Sometimes the honey trap had its compensations. He was powerful, much more powerful than she'd thought. His hands cradled her head and before she could react he snapped her neck as easily as one of the breadsticks they'd enjoyed in the restaurant earlier. Her legs buckled and he lowered Sam's lifeless body gently and quietly to the floor. No blood, no mess, no trace. Nathan sent the one word text message to summon the team that would collect and dispose of Sam's body. Nothing remained to suggest that Sam had ever been with Nathan in room 601.

Just because Sam had left the service didn't mean that over the years they hadn't kept their eye on her and her activities. These, they now judged, had become a source of potential embarrassment to the service and to those in grey suits who had first recruited her. To them Sam's life was no more or no less than a commodity; a commodity which, for them, no longer held a value… and so they ended it.

Christmas 1951

My maternal grandmother's Victorian house, a three storey, red brick, mid terrace with a large bay front, was a shrine to tobacco smoke and pine disinfectant. Three well-worn, well-scrubbed, stone steps led up from the pavement, its exterior offering no clues as to the shadow laden labyrinth concealed within. A heavy, windowless, bottle green coloured front door opened onto the intricately tiled floor of the vestibule; its leaded, stained glass inner door, a portal to endless stairs, locked off spaces and long, lino covered hallways with high ceilings. The latched, black door, under the stairs, concealed a claustrophobic plunge into the menace of the dank cellar below. This foreboding space was in stark contrast to the bright, spacious attic room, with its curtain less windows, at the top of the house.

Christmas celebrations were in full swing and the volume of the music, laughter and conversations ebbed and flowed with the opening and closing of the door to the front lounge. The first floor bedroom, immediately above, was cavernous in daylight but now, midway through this party evening, appeared infinitely larger; lit only by the soft, sepia glow of a thin wedge of landing light that struggled to squeeze past the slightly open bedroom door. Perimeters lost their definition as they withdrew into the infinite darkness and grey on black undefined, unwelcome shadows appeared, unheralded, from out of nowhere only to melt away just as silently into an unknown nothingness. Persistent heavy rain rattled the net curtained, sash windows while outside, suspended, wind-blown streetlights bobbed like strung up apples on Halloween. Below them the road of rained on, regimented, granite sets glistened wet and mosaic like, reflecting rainbow colours.

The last thing I remembered, as I drifted off to sleep, was the song,

'Some enchanted evening', from the musical 'South Pacific', playing on the gramophone one floor below. I don't know how much later it was but I awoke with a start; there was something on my bed and it was moving; it was alive! More than scared I was terrified as I felt the fearless, unseen thing confidently exploring the quilted eiderdown, under which I'd been so peacefully sleeping. My single bed occupied one corner of the room, adjacent to the window wall and parallel to the partially open door. In an instant I'd backed up against and was pressing hard into the union of the heavily varnished headboard and floral papered wall. The surface struck ice cold against my back as it overwhelmed the scant protection offered by the brushed cotton of my pyjamas. In automatic response to the uninvited presence, the cause of my wide-eyed terror, I scrunched together, in white knuckle grips, my satin quilted eiderdown, hairy blanket and smooth sheet as, defensively, I pulled them all up beneath my quivering chin; my breathing now rapid and faltering.

I was four years old; I cried out and I yelled, of course I did, but the grown-ups couldn't have heard me, because not one of them climbed the stairs to investigate my distress calls. Molten tears spilled down my cheeks as I tried, in vain, to make myself heard over the revelry below. Water filled eyes further distorted whatever amorphous shapes I could make out in the poor light. Four years may not be a long time to some but to me they constituted the entirety of my young life. I couldn't remember ever making more noise than this; and still no one came. Unopposed, the 'thing' continued its silent survey of my bed. I knew absolutely that it was only a matter of time before it would see for itself the undeniable fear in my wide, rubbed red eyes. I felt it as it moved about; I felt it when it paused and then, as it shifted up and down on the same spot, deliberately taunting as well as petrifying me, I felt it.

In time the seemingly bottomless well, from which my tears had so readily sprung, ran itself dry and the pleading cries and shouts of an eternity receded, giving way to shuddering, almost silent sobs that racked and pained my small body. I was empty and my throat hurt, it had dried up and I found it sore and difficult to swallow, even if I'd summoned up the courage to do so; for now that I was quiet I was afraid 'the thing' would hear me.

I didn't understand; questions raced around my young mind, questions which, nearly sixty five years later, I can't recall verbatim. However, if today, as an adult, I was asking those same questions, the words I'd use would be something like,

'I've made enough noise so why doesn't someone, anyone, come and save me from this thing that's terrifying me? Perhaps they've forgotten about me or maybe they just don't care? Could it be they don't love me enough to take a break from their revelry, if only for a few minutes, to come and check on me?' Reluctantly I'd conclude, 'That's it; they just don't love me enough to care!'

Then, from out of nowhere, a great commotion; the bedroom door crashed open and anonymous figures were rushing towards me, at first haloed by, and then blocking out the landing light. In an instant someone swept me up into their arms and held me tight as they cuddled and swayed me to and fro, shushing me, telling me in whispered, reassuring tones, 'It's alright now' and 'There, there baby, oh darling, please don't cry'. Relief at finally being rescued tapped a new well and brought forth once more a cascade of stinging, burning tears. Now, it seemed, they all wanted to gently stroke my white blonde curls, to comfort and calm me as they competed to cradle me; I'd become the living prize in a pass the parcel competition. But, I was safe at last and the ironically named 'Mephi', short for Mephistopheles, the family's enormous, black tomcat, the great beast that had reigned such terror, was quickly banished from my bed forever but regretfully not from my dreams; for in these it would return to stalk and terrorise me, night after night, down the years.

Mystery on the 18C

My time as a bus conductor taught me a lot, but two things in particular; the first was that there was no legislating for the actions or utterances of the passengers who rode my bus and secondly that the unexpected was a measure only of my own inexperience. So it was, just after daybreak one bleak winter's morning in the mid 1960s, that as I collected fares on the top deck of an old back loader, senses were assaulted and sensibilities advanced. So early was the hour that most of the seats were empty and as is usual, when given the choice, the passengers were displaying 'DWRS', 'Doctor's Waiting Room Syndrome', and had taken up residence as far away from each other as was possible, even if it meant shivering, as they eschewed the benefits of collective body heat in the hopes of completing their respective journeys without the need to share with another *their* space, *their* territory and *their* uncomfortable, thinly cushioned, leatherette upholstered, bench seat. What's more, the displeasure of some was obvious and often audible when a fellow traveller boarded and had the audacity, the temerity to encroach upon *their* own special place. Proof, to me, not that any proof was needed, that millennia of social engineering and some oft voiced religious tenets such as *'love thy neighbour'*, for these passengers at least and on this bitterly cold morning in particular, had been seeds sown on stony ground. People were still half asleep, dozing with tired, squinting eyes straining against the harsh brightness of the interior lights. Some, with heads resting on cold windows, turned for relief to the darkness outside and the more gentle light of dawn. Perhaps stark reflections of reality clashed with the cushioned make-believe of recently abandoned dreams, as sleep fought to snatch them back from reality and their new day.

I heard and felt, before seeing, the monster in the dirty, navy boiler suit. It seemed that his every crashing step on the metal, spiral stairs caused the old bus to slowly roll, first right and then left, right and then left. Only on his reaching the top of the stairs did I appreciate the monster's true size. On reflection, 'appreciate', seems an inappropriate way to describe my immediate emotions and I guessed it wouldn't have been the first choice of word for many of those in attendance, those who had been so rudely roused and had turned, curious at the commotion. Standing at least six foot six inches tall and tipping the scales, I guessed, at a minimum of twenty five stone (c.160 kg) this was indeed a monster of biblical proportions. I'm sure I heard at least one passenger praying for deliverance. My own words, "Holy shit!", although loud in my head, never escaped clenched teeth behind sealed lips. The monster and his dirty boiler suit could have easily won first prizes in *'Spot the Stain'* and *'Guess the Smell'* competitions or been the pin up on the front cover of *'Sewerage Workers Weekly'*. Breathing hard he paused at the top of the stairs and deliberately collected the glances of the unfortunate few who'd been unable to avert their gazes quickly enough; those who now ruefully remembered the old saying, something about curiosity killing the cat. Lowering his huge bull-like head, unintentionally fashionable with its dirt caked, matted dreadlocks, he hunched his back and made his way towards me. I, wishing to extend my usual courtesy to this passenger, as I would to any other of course, backed into an empty seat, forced a smile and as I ushered him by made a mental note to request, at the next union branch meeting, that shotguns and body armour become standard issue for me and my brother bus conductors. I would have raised a drawbridge had there been one, indeed had there been time I'd have built one. As he passed me, squeezing down the aisle, giant mud encrusted boots left inch high crumbling tyre tread deposits with each restricted step.

With the whole of the upper deck virtually empty there was a large selection of unoccupied seats from which he could have chosen. However, rather than picking one of the vacant seats the monster lurched forward and with a huge sigh slumped down to his right, next to an attractive, slightly built, well dressed, young woman in her early twenties. The trapped air in the sponge cushion hissed loudly as it objected to being so abruptly and forcibly expelled through stitch holes in the backside buffed leatherette. The bench seat was barely big enough for him alone and his young involuntary travelling companion instantly recoiled from his uninvited presence, moving over as far as she could towards the window without actually leaving by it. Perhaps her reaction was prompted by the fact that the monster and his overalls were more than a little smelly and dirty. Maybe his not inconsiderable size intimidated her, or, I wondered, could it just have been the question that must surely have sprung into her head,

'With all these empty seats why has he chosen to sit next to me?'

Side by side they made a truly incongruous pair; a modern day Beauty and the Beast.

As I approached the couple a loud and rumbling fart rent the air asunder, shattering the early morning peace and comatose tranquillity of the upper deck. The young woman seemed to retreat even further, into a space between her and the window that didn't in fact exist. A few seconds later the big man dropped his right shoulder, tilted his head towards her and without looking directly at her, in a deep and gravelled voice attempted an intimate whisper; one that was heard by all on the top deck, if not the whole bus,

'Don't worry girl… they'll think it was me!'

In an instant the young woman was on her feet, as if stung by a cattle prod. Flushed and visibly shaking she somehow managed to scramble past the big man and then me before making a stumbling, hasty exit along the aisle, her stiletto heels clattering, staccato like, down the corkscrew stairs.

In the absence of a denial from the young woman I don't know whether she had cause to be embarrassed by the words of the big man in the boiler suit. Neither I, nor anyone else on the top deck, could be absolutely certain as to the originator of the audible and now olfactory detected emission. No one was going to ask either contender if they were the perpetrator, not the young woman, as she'd fled the bus, and certainly not the monster in the dirty, navy boiler suit, for the obvious but understandable consideration of self-preservation… The true identity of the culprit, therefore, remains a mystery to this day.

Unexpected

I'd settled for the expected and so
the impact of you hit me all the harder.
I shattered and crashed like old glass
and my weathered, cobwebbed frame is
once more exposed to emotion's elements.
Dull, safe patterns, that decorated life,
at best lay broken and meaningless.
Your beautiful impossibilities now dazzle
and beckon, inviting me to believe,
daring me to dream, expecting me to live,
...caring.

Nigel Irving

What I write

I suppose it's a range of stuff. Some is childhood recollections and the strange characters from that vanished world of the 60's. Then some is from later as a young man out and about in the pubs and clubs of Liverpool. I reckon I pick up on some of the people I have met and try to recall them so as they're not forgotten in the mists of time.

Descent to Chaos. 1965.

It was a strange sight for a nine year old boy. It was surreal if I'd known that word then.

My dad in our living room, standing to attention to the National Anthem. I hadn't been well (again) and had slept on the couch all afternoon, so I was still awake when BBC One ended. I had watched with monumental disinterest the news, national then local and then the epilogue which seemed to involve a vicar telling you off.

Then suddenly up he went like Alec Guinness in *Bridge on the River Kwai*. He was standing to attention as God Save the Queen played us out. He never said anything and neither did my Mum, who never stood up. In fact, she never actually looked up. She was reading a book called *The Carpetbaggers* and stubbing her cigarette out. She took no notice at all. I wondered what that book was about. I wasn't allowed to look at it and when my mother wasn't reading it just disappeared and never returned to the bookcase. My dad said it was a load of cobblers and she should read a proper book like *The Cruel Sea.*

Immediately as it ended, he got two fag ends out the ashtray. He put one behind his ear and the other in his breast pocket. Then he said, "He's right you know, Eileen."

"Who is?" said my mum.

"Alf Garnett in that programme before, *Till Death Us Do Part*. They should never of let this bloody crowd in. They turn up here, can't speak the language, next thing you know they're down the Labour exchange."

"He's not a real person, Jack; I've told you before he's a caricature of a cockney East End working class man who just happens to be a bigot. Just like you, which is why you like him. Same as that other fella."

"Who?"

"Ian Paisley, that's who, bloody trouble maker he is."

My Nan walked in from the kitchen with a large glass of Teachers whiskey with hot water in it. "Ian Paisley," she said. "I'll not have that man's name mentioned in my house."

"Well it's not your house is it, its mine - and so is that whiskey."

"Ooh, my poor Fred was right about you. You wouldn't say that if he was here today."

"Well he's not, is he? The lucky sod."

My mums attention was drawn by this harmless remark. "Don't you take my father's name in vain! You're not fit to lace his boots."

"He always said you should have married George," my nan said.

"Yes he did, Mum – and now he's editor of the *Liverpool Echo*."

"Not a plumber's mate," Nan added.

"Well, we all know how he made his money, paying the poor bugger's that worked for him starvation wages, while he lived the life of Riley."

Nan was now in the guise of profound shock, hand to mouth.

"How dare you! He worked himself into the grave, my Fred. He was a proper business man and a gentleman. Not like your father."

They were moving in for the kill. The resentful faces, the pointing fingers. The circle of hate was closing. My mum lighting a cigarette, ghostly and menacing behind a vale of smoke.

"Oh I remember it well; no one knew what happened to him. Just disappeared, he did, until that phone call from your sister in Vancouver."

My dad was slumped in his chair sulking, waiting for the punch line I guessed he had heard many times before. His final attempt of defence floundering as he mumbled, "He was a chief engineer with Holder Brothers Line."

Mum stood up now. "Was he indeed? Well, it didn't stop him falling off the ship drunk as a lord in the Panama Canal!"

"He was a scoundrel," Nan added.

"He was well paid."

"Well, your mother never saw any of it. Not unless she wanted to be a cleaner in Walton Hospital."

"Leave my mother out of it. She was a wonderful woman."

"She had enough practice, six kids one after the other."

My Nan dealt the killer blow. Quietly spoken and below the belt as ever, "I've never seen children look so different."

"You watch it, you! You're in my house, remember."

"Not by choice," she threw in.

"Well, it's not my choice either! And another thing, where did you get that nose from? Ha Greenwood. Greenberg it was till the old fella changed it. You're Jewish, you are. I don't know how Hitler missed you."

"How dare you?" came in female unison.

He was in full flow now. “The only way your husband got anywhere was because of his cronies at the Anfield Masonic Lodge.”

“He was a very influential man. Anyway, they all helped each other.”

“He never helped anyone in his whole life, except himself – and certainly not me. He was the meanest man I’ve ever met. You’d die of thirst waiting for him to buy a drink.”

Mum closed her book. “Right, I’ve heard enough. I’m going to bed. You get in with me mum.”

“Suit yourself.” Utterly aghast, he turned to me, “And you get to bed, Nigel. As far as I can see there’s bugger all wrong with you.”

He looked diminished, smaller than the tiny dot at the centre of the television set.

A few weeks later Nan moved to a flat around the corner to us. She never liked it and ended up in Ormskirk hospital after a stroke. Strangely enough, my dad used to go and see her, on his push bike mostly, or the train if it was raining.

My mum said she couldn’t set foot in that place again. “Not after she’d had everything taken away there.”

Eventually Nan went back to the flat, with nurses calling twice a day. I was playing football in the street one Saturday afternoon when I saw Dad coming round the corner pushing Nan in her wheelchair. All wrapped up in a tartan blanket. It was a funny sight, the two of them gliding down the road with a trail of cigarette smoke behind them.

I could hear them talking as they passed by. My nan waving to me with her good arm.

“Yes, Ma, we’ll stick the old racing on and have a scotch. It’s Doncaster and Haydock on ITV. We can pick, have a bet if you like, I’ve got the Express in the house. Pick a few out and I’ll have a walk over.”

“Ooh, that would be lovely, Jackie,” Nan said.

I helped Dad lift the wheelchair over the step and into the hall. I came back about two hours later to see the football results. They were both asleep with the television still on and two empty glasses on the coffee table. I suppose they had made their peace. My Nan let the flat go and stayed with us. She died in the winter of 1971 in our back bedroom. The same bedroom my Dad died in fifteen years later almost to the day.

Dickens' Ghost

In shadows grey, he moves through memories of his life,
under the cast iron arch at Southwark Bridge.
The children of the streets emerge,
alone again at Hungerford Stairs,

Or not alone, defiant Nancy,
redeemed her soul upon these steps.
She weeps for Fagin, for which there is no reason,
save the spirit lost.

To hellfire and its wrath,
still he walks these ever changing streets.
The world is strange now,
his time and fashion gone.

There is room for him on the crowded pavement,
unseen and formless.
Yet succumbed to darkness,
perhaps to seek a lost love?

Or suffer nightly, on this wrack of passion,
to make an end of things.
Slipping quietly to the dark waters.
he was a man who may not think it right.

To ever slip from earthly sight,
able to describe the human heart.
Condemned to others from the very start,
the night walks carry him light.

Take supper at the inn that bears his name,
where once he lingered, and was known to be.
Held in thrall, so they would like him well.

I am set against the virtues I have known,
my skin is loose my body worn.
All fallen to decay and worse,
called back to life.

I walk again, fast and far
from Middlesex Ridge to Blackfriar Bridge
and beyond to my old home;.
no measure of him

Save a windchime, that tinkled
his faultless exit.
Somewhere at the worlds end
a cone of light dimmed.

The Gypsy Woman

She walked our path each summer
peddling pegs and rag dolls.
Passed almost silent, just creaking bone
and dreaded stare. Her eyes grey shutters
to the past, perhaps the future.
She had no shadow.
Her voice shrill, like birdsong
in a birdless sky.
She bore a quilt, in a wicker bag.
It smelt of roses, mice and bottled wine.
It had a memory of Autumn woodsmoke.
and canal men
in highway gowns;
like Turpin's ghost,
dangling from a branch,
fruit flies at his final breath.

Mourned by deathly maidens
on some sleepy lane,
his death mask sold for a coin.
Yet, she disappeared in tail water,
like an otter, as though perished.
We sing her name, in taverns,
like a ballad.
Somewhere in that wild silence
she heard a bell, distinct.
And so she passed,
like all the seasons she had watched.
like that quilt, she lay on to die.
Stilled by the world itself,
gone to the world beyond.

Unsaveable

The first conversation.

I want an island, tropical at least.
I want to dream myself a beach.
All those things I cannot have
and cannot reach

Part One.

Wildcat Lisa, she knows the night is falling.
But her life won't wait,
for this night to pass
by its blood cut birth,

She left her soul
in the ash of men.

"Remember me," she said,
"if you don't see me again."

But her love song
dimmed to whispers, and no hope left.
Humbled to drama,
more splendid than life.

And not for a long time,
did she feel the cut of the knife.
The skin opened up, an artery tore,
a litre of blood
on the cell floor.

And the jailhouse screamed.
through the prison night.
When the torchlight shone,
its circle of light.

On a stage of her own,
in a dream that was over.
She became the world through which she'd passed,
a blessed undoing, in obsolete form.

Part Two.
When we talked all night,
but it's just the same.
Only the time and date remain.

I watched her in that single moment
fall to gloom.
Where none could reach
herself to save.

With the night's slow sweep.
the darkness took her ten fathoms deep.

I'll walk tonight, and not faint hearted.
Pass that room,
where deathless shadows wait.

All dulled to grief and memory.
and so her name means nothing now;
except to me – perhaps some other,
who sit alone, at midnight's hour

to call her back again.
But only her words come back,
slow retainers of my chaotic failure.
Her notion of love,

unreturnable,
at this time or in this place.
And so instead, requested as my friend
that she could stay, if courage ran to surplus.

And her reply.
"My friend would never ask me
to live in hell without purpose."

The words that were never said.
"And I will see you there my love,
where the palm trees sway
and the sun shines golden, at the end of every day."

"Where the night will never find you
and all before you past.
On that beach you dreamed of,
home again at last."

Vanessa Louise Lester

What I write

I dabble in drabble. I curse in verse. I mash the flash. I pose in prose. I play at plays and I kill with my pen again and again.

But most of all, I spend my days, my nights, with words that swim, that float inside my head. That wake me up when I'm in bed.

With words that do nothing much when all alone but placed with others, become a script or a poem.

With words that paint both dark and light, these words I write, for all who read to see, these words forever; a part of me.

Carousel

The aged door hangs from a rusted hinge
and tired splintered rotten frame.
Faded rainbow paint-flecks
dance on the sea breeze
like kites, from summers gone.
Memories float like foam waves
Kiss me quick ice cream lips.
Fish and chips, snatched
by greedy thieving gulls.
Tinny tunes waltz the carousel
Boom bump screech beep boom
Sticky fingers wipe the candy sugared tears.
Salty smiles, then frowns
as grain by grain, that never ending war
of castle against shore
is lost again, again, again
Shifting tides that turn
that twist, that rain
that batter to shades of stormy grey.
The boom of sea now all.

The aged door hangs from a silver shiny hinge.
Replacement joints
that creak alive once more,
to calming waves, that rest upon the shore.
Fixed up. Patched up. Nearly new.
Reconditioned.
Patchwork paint
of red white and blue.
That déjà vu, of twists of turns of
tinny tunes that twist
that turn, that waltz, the carousel.
Boom bump screech beep boom.
Hold tight, those moments never lost

transferred, passed on. A gift from
mothers, fathers, daughter, son.
This gift of memories to come
Hold tight, those moments grain by grain
Hold tight.
Our dizzy summers come
Again, again, again.

Everything will be ok

Our lives packed up, scaled down, crammed,
contained in lorry then in boat. Suffocating heat,
then paralysing cold.
I say "Everything will be ok"
With a reassuring smile, from mouth not eyes.
The worst is over. But I do not know.
if worse is yet to come. Penned in.
In lorry, then in boat, that smells of rotten flesh
not fish. That bobs upon the sea, on wave, on estuary.
That bobs to port that turns away.
They're scared. So I say "Everything will be ok"
With a reassuring smile, from mouth not eyes.
I wipe away their salty tears,
their cries. From mouth. From eyes.
And then, penned in,
in lorry, boat and train, another place again,
that won't know what to do. With us. With them.
They're scared, they say. They want to go back home.
So I say "everything will be ok."
With a reassuring smile from mouth not eyes, because I do not know
If worse is yet to come.
I hide my salty tears, my fears, my lies.
From mouth. From eyes.

Our lives contained. In trains, on platforms where it rains,
exposed, on view, like animals in a zoo.
We wait. We queue. Accused. In news.
We're hungry, they say. We want a place to stay.
So I say "Everything will be ok".
With a reassuring smile from mouth not eyes, because
I do not know if worse is yet to come. So tired. So now I cannot hide,
no matter how I try, these lies, the tears, my fears.
From mouth. From eyes.

The Attic

I lie on the wooden floorboards, trying to catch particles dancing in sunbeams through rafters. Too quick for my fingers, these living atoms that surround us, rarely seen not for what they truly are, anyway.

"Tom, are you here?" He appears, unsmiling, his tatty trousers and baggy white shirt just as I remembered.

"Don't be moody." I tickle his ribs. He giggles and lies next to me.

We had been friends ever since I could remember. The attic was my hideaway, our place.

"I miss you, Libby"

This time was for good. They'd sold the house. I was going away, university, leaving Tom forever.

My throat tightened. Through my tears, I see my soul dancing in sunbeams.

* * *

When they had viewed the house Sarah hadn't felt anything. Now she shivered every time she walked past the attic. Just her imagination playing tricks, like Jack's new 'friends' Tom and Libby.

Day 20330: A Fleeting Moment

When he was sure no one was watching, he folded the umbrella, raised his head to the swirling clouds, raindrops danced from closed eyelids to chin.

It had rained on their last night. Warm torrential explosions, parting waves, crashing thunder beats onto the white sands of Koh Rok.

"Let's find cover."

His hand lost hers, as he moved towards the trees. He turned, saw she was laughing, naked, the sodden dress at her feet. Wet, hungry kisses, fingers locked, they walked into the sea.

She dived in, teasing him, white foam crowning her black hair. Bodies submerged, became merged. Both changed forever.

He didn't know why she wasn't there when he left. He knew something had happened. Stopped her.

6764 days had passed. He had moved from city to town, searching. He didn't stay anywhere long but when he told his story they looked at him oddly. 3 days together.20330 he had lived. Time had stopped for him that day.

He stood smiling, waiting till the rain stopped.

* * *

She spun, arms outstretched, grey hairs glistening in the lightning strobe. She loved storms. She wondered if he ever thought of her. He was her first thought when she awoke 6761 days ago and last at night. She knew they find each other again.

My Dance

This time was different. I was flying but not dancing. That point between sleep and waking, pirouetting wildly through clouds, floating adagio over streams of air. I felt alive, free, exhilarated. My dance.

I had asked others if they dreamed that way. They told me no, they did not dream. They did not have the time. I laughed. Everyone dreams! Maybe they just couldn't remember.

This time was different. My arms jerked uncontrolled ugly rhythm. The dance of a marionette. Rising slowly, upwards, leg aloft, arabesque, I saw others, pulled in various directions by near invisible wire. All succumbed gracefully, eyes shut, hooked by an invisible master. Except me. My chains tugged, yanked harder, staining white wool clouds with blood rain. My silent screams of pain unheard.

Exhausted, I could fight no more.

I now understood why others do not dream. I knew I would not dance my dance again.

The Tempest

Even though it was expected, I jumped when the knock came.

Dirt tears lined her worried face. A man behind her, held the child in his arms.

"Please help us, we have travelled far."

She held out a gold coin. I knew she had more.

"It is late Madam." I opened the door anyway, gesturing entry.

The child began screaming, writhing, shouting words alien to us all.

Struggling to keep hold, he placed her on the floor.

"The devil is in her, can you help?"

"It is bad. Really bad. You must leave her here tonight. The price is 10 gold sovereigns"

The woman tried to protest but he passed me the money bag before she could speak.

"It is all we have."

When they had left, I called my tempest back into the jar.

As the child slept peacefully, I wondered where I should place it next.

The Clockmaker

I wasn't sure whether to be irritated or impressed that he had tracked me down. This guy had the patience of a saint and I've met many. His 26,245 hours, 45 minutes and 26 seconds of searching left him in need of a hot bath.

The Clockmaker has always been my preferred name. Beautiful and intricate, their beating tick tocks give them a life of their own. I am maker, occasional repairer, but when their pendulum stops completely, nothing can be done.

I knew why he was here, the bargain, to increase her time by giving up his. He loved her more than life itself. As I met his stare, I nodded. He mouthed "Thank you."

When she awoke, she read his letter. Doctors claimed miracle but it was short lived. After 3 years of coma, her heart simply stopped.

Sadly time cannot always be fixed, even by a Clockmaker.

The Office Christmas Party

Chris Klaus had booked a table at San Carlos for the office Christmas party. This was one of the most expensive and pretentious restaurants in the city centre. He had booked it for 30 but only two people had bothered to come. Jim Kelly his number two and Elsie his office manager, who he would have retired off years ago, but the reality was, she knew too much.

Also if he was honest with himself, he found it difficult to manage if she took an hour lunch, never mind a holiday, but in the 40 years he had known her, she rarely did.

"I don't understand it." Chris shook his head as he poured himself another glass of red.

"I wouldn't have got where I am today if I'd looked a gift horse in the mouth."

"Miserable sods, the lot of them," agreed Jim as he shovelled another overflowing spoon of zabaglione into his nicotine stained mouth. Chris looked at Jim, and made a mental note that next year he was not going to sit by him at the Christmas do.

Elsie peered at her boss through glasses perched precariously on her pointed noise and decided the time had nearly come. She grabbed the bottle of red and filled his glass up to the top.

“Maybe asking the staff for a £30.00 contribution, when they haven’t received a Christmas bonus this year was a mistake, Mr Klaus?”

Mr Klaus tried to focus across the table in the direction of Elsie’s voice. She said so little usually that he wondered if he had just imagined it. He made another mental note to check how much sherry was on the final bill.

“We are in a recession, Elsie. We have all had to tighten our belts. There is no such thing as a free lunch, or should that be free Christmas night out anymore?” He snorted at the hilarity of his own joke until Jim, a second or two late, said a little too loudly, “Ho Ho Ho,” and rubbed his massive belly as he did so. By the looks of him, Jim had loosened his belt.

“I mean, profits are down again this year, so what do they expect?” slurred Chris, as Jim nodded approvingly, his mouth full of cheese.

Elsie said nothing and filled up the men’s glasses again. Chris, not liking the silence, felt the need to fill it.

“Anyway, Elsie, what are your plans for Christmas?”

“The usual, Mr Klaus, dinner at the nursing home with Mum,” replied Elsie, knowing that he wasn’t really interested.

Chris noticed that Elsie seemed to be swaying. Or was it him swaying? He was confused. Elsie had a mum but Elsie must be nearly 80. Why didn’t he know that Elsie still had a mum? This was not good. He might end up stuck with Elsie for another 20 years if longevity ran in the family.

Chris poured himself another glass of red and wondered what to say next. He really wished that one of his companions would speak, rather than him having to make all the effort. Next year he would cancel Christmas. All this fuss over one day in the calendar. It was bad enough that he had to pay staff when they weren’t working. He always went into the office on the 25th December unless it fell on a Sunday. That was why he had got where he was today.

The bill had appeared on the table. “Did I ask for that?” wondered Chris, as he examined the bill, which would have been easier to do had the numbers stayed still. He noticed that Elsie and Jim had put their £30.00

contribution onto the plate. There was no sherry on the bill, and he surmised that Elsie may have a sneaky bottle in her handbag.

The waiter brought over the card machine, as Chris pocketed the £60.00 and paid the bill which included service, so there was no need to tip. He made sure he got his VAT receipt and the waiter smiled unconvincingly as he brought it over.

Chris woke with a start the next day and checked his watch. It said Sat, 2.00pm. He checked to see where he was and was relieved to find himself in his own king size bed and alone. His head hurt. 2.00 pm? How did that happen? He vaguely remembered leaving the restaurant, Elsie linking him and chattering away as he walked. She must have had more sherry than he had thought. Was she holding him up or was he holding her? He couldn't be one hundred percent sure but it may have been a bit of both. He remembered going to the office. It hadn't been late, about 9.30pm but he couldn't for the life him remember anything else.

He felt sick. In the last 40 years he had only had one day off work ill. That's a lot more than could be said for his staff who always seemed to have some family emergency or something going on. He left Elsie to sort out that type of thing. Sod it, he thought, I am going to have a Saturday off.

He stumbled out of bed and made himself a cup of coffee and searched in his cupboards for some Ibuprofen. He turned on the TV and flicked over and over the channels but couldn't find anything to watch. He checked his book shelf and didn't see anything he fancied. He was bored. Why couldn't he remember getting home last night? He had a nagging feeling that something had happened and wondered whether he should ring Elsie, but he knew she went somewhere on Saturdays. Probably to see her mother. Why had he not known she had a mother?

He spent most of the weekend in bed. He hated Sundays, but he wouldn't have got to where he was today, had he not ensured he had at least one day a week away from the office. Monday was Christmas Eve. There had been requests that the office should close but he had not agreed. Christmas Eve was not a bank holiday and they lost enough working days at this time of year.

He arrived at the office on Monday promptly at 9.00 am. He suspected as usual that he would be greeted by grumpy faces of staff who wanted to be elsewhere but as he walked in the main entrance he noticed that reception had been decorated with tinsel and tree had placed in the corner. Had he approved decorations from petty cash? Tina, his receptionist, wearing a Santa hat and flashing bauble earrings, gave him huge smile and said, “Good morning Mr Klaus,” in a way that made him feel a little disconcerted.

As he walked into the main office, he was greeted with a round of applause. The office sparkled with tinsel and there didn’t seem to be any work surface not covered with a decoration or two. He didn’t like this. Why was everyone clapping? My God, they are singing now. *For He’s a Jolly Good Fellow,* surely they didn’t mean him? He rushed through to his office and closed the door to hide from them. Was he dreaming?

He rang through to Elsie and demanded she came in. “What the hell is going on?” Elsie smiled. “The staff just wanted to show you their appreciation, Mr Klaus, for the bonus and the email you sent them, you have been truly generous.” What bonus? What email?

He checked his emails. He saw bank confirmation of various transfers but couldn’t work out why. He checked his sent items. Friday 21.52. All users. Subject. I wouldn’t be where I am today without my staff.

I have decided to operate a profit share bonus to all staff based on length of service. Whilst profits are down, we are still making profit and plenty of it. I realised today that things must be difficult for some of my staff. No pay rises for 3 years, no bonus schemes and higher mortgage payments. I don’t have family of my own and I consider Klaus and Co as my family, so I have divided £1.5 million profits between you all. May I take this opportunity to wish you all a very Merry Christmas and a Happy New Year.

P.S. I have taken the decision to close at 1.00 pm Christmas Eve and not to reopen until the 2nd January.

Chris stared open mouthed at the screen. “Get me the security cameras…Now!” he shouted. He felt sick again. He looked again at the bank transfers. Surely the bank would have done security checks. How did someone hack his computer? How did they hack the banks computer? Elsie returned with the security discs and placed the first one into his disc drive. At exactly 21.36 the rear door showed both him and Elsie. Elsie appeared to be holding him up. She was still chattering away by the looks of it. “Jesus,” he thought, she did get loose tongued after a drink. She put the key in the door and helped him into the building, and then turned and exited through the door, leaving him alone in the office. Elsie removed the first disc. The second disc showed him walking alone through the main office and as he did so he did a little dance in front of the camera.

Chris stared at the screen. He appeared again 30 minutes later wearing a Santa hat possibly the same one that Tina greeted him with this morning and a box load of Christmas decorations. He watched amazed as he saw himself decorating the main office stopping every few minutes or so to do another little dance. “My God, it looks like I’m singing,” he said out loud. Elsie smiled.

White faced, he turned the computer off. “I don’t remember a thing,” he said, as his mind raced thinking about how he could demand the return of his money. If he hadn’t seen himself with his own eyes he would never have believed it. Never would he drink red wine again.

Elsie patted him on the shoulder. “There, there, Mr Klaus - as you always say, ‘I wouldn’t have got where I am today, if I didn’t stick to the decisions I make.’ Enjoy it, a happy workforce is a productive one and I don’t think I have ever seen such a happy workforce, in all my years.”

Chris Klaus smiled weakly as the staff one by one wished him a happy Christmas and thanked him for his generosity. Elsie explained to them that he didn’t want a fuss and was embarrassed by all the attention. He watched over the CCTV again and again, but still no memories of Friday night returned.

As Elsie left she wished Mr Klaus a Happy Christmas and told him if he was at a loose end he was welcome to join her and Mum at the home for some Christmas turkey. She couldn’t quite catch what he said as his head was in his hands, but she would ring him later, to remind him.

As the longest standing employee, Elsie had done very well out of this bonus scheme. She would probably return to work though as, apart from her mother, she had no one else and she really did think of Klaus and Co as her extended family.

With her money, and New Year coming up, she might pick a new part time course - a language course this time. She could afford a little holiday now but probably wouldn’t go for too long. Mr Klaus didn’t like it when she was off.

Yes, a new course was the answer and would keep her busy. She felt that she had gone as far as she could now with the hypnotherapy course that she had done every Saturday for the last few years.

Room 101

Attached to a wooden fob, the room key is too bulky for a purse, but small enough to lose in a cluttered handbag, Numbers 101 are etched in patchy gold, without humour or irony.

The door opens into a tight walkthrough. A bare magnolia wall on the left, mock mahogany fitted wardrobes to the right that house 'His and Hers' bathrobes which drape over a barely used trouser press.

The heavy door shuts in slow motion and is papered with bold emergency instructions IN CASE OF FIRE. The 'Do not disturb,' sign swings flimsily from the handle as it closes.

Adjacent to the wardrobe, the bathroom door is panelled in frosted glass, through which the silhouette of the toilet can be seen.

And heard.

A room to be shared only by those with no illusions left.

The bath, too big for one but cramped for two. The surrounding tiles are beige with a hint of coffee, except under the shower, where the water has carved pale orange stains that cannot be removed by chamber maids with elbow grease.

A hairdryer, thief proofed, curly flexed is fixed to a socket next to the shaving plug above the sink. The mirror is strategically placed, spotlights blown dark. Sitting on the glass shelf are the freebies. Corporate branded, usually unused but always taken home on principle. The towels are worn but clean. The cardboard signs in green beg for help to 'Save Our Planet.'

The walkthrough opens wide to reveal a king sized bed covered brilliant white, with a quilted chocolate throw at the foot. The headboard and arm chairs continue the many shades of brown. A Jackson Pollock print hangs awkwardly against the inoffensive, hollow wall that echoes each restless night through the mirror image room next door.

The sideboard holds the TV that comes with added extras, and hides the empty fridge. The traditional mini bar has been replaced by lobby vending machines. Something old, something new, nothing borrowed, till payments made.

A basket of many flavoured sachets, plastic UHT cartons and never enough biscuits, are served on a tray which rests on a 70's flat pack writing desk, in keeping with the sideboard and the wardrobe, more Princess Ann than Queen. The hotel paper and pen hide, forgotten, underneath the laminated 'Free Wifi' instructions. The kettle holds enough for two small cups, and has a sticker confirming that it's a 'safe and tested appliance.'

The windows open - just. Locks fitted keep burglars and fresh air out, keep children and smokers in, preventing the urge to dangle above the industrial steel bins of the kitchen below.

This room makes do for all and pleases few. This room, the same as all the rest, but different. A patch, a spot, a splatter, in other shades of brown, missed by the deep clean, missed by forensics, uncovered by replacement carpet. A patch, a spot, a splatter, out of view, but there, behind a radiator, making this a room that will always be unique, that will never quite be as it was before.

Annmarie Lowther

What I write

I write the idea that curls and whets around the corners to keep me from sleep. I trace the pictures that bloom from outline to colour with the sound turned down. Then I wait and listen for the unheard, sundered voice before it fades, sinking back into silence. Sometimes the indelible is caught between the words, like a warm breath in the cold air, only visible to me. Maybe it shouts, or hides, screams or pants or whispers; maybe it is not worth the effort, but that is what I write, before the next serrated, copper-bright image turns my head.

Woman Obscured

In the ladies at Euston Station
I turned to look at the woman
washing her feet
in the hand basin,
like Magdalen bowed to Christ.

At first she bathed her heels
then roved, haste-less, upwards:
ankles, knees, shoulders,
breeched. There beneath brown curls,
denuded, no girls face.

Plain strong flour turned
to a fresh bread offering;
scattered age lines
less sunburn splinters
A well-fed mona lisa abroad

She pulled on her socks, woollen
and thick,
Pushed down her skirts,
Slipped swollen feet into
White hulled sandals.

As if re-assembling herself, part by
Part, stealth of
Cloth. Order reinstated
layer by layer.
Unaware amidst the bustle,

Looking Inwards, carefully.
The last movement
Of the symphony
of mystery:

gold braid edges
white leather tips
earthen chiffon
thickening waist
burly legged
fall of curls,
the burka slipped over her head.

Cusp

That soft space behind your ear
Redolent of tender care
Now fleeting as you slip away
With downy lip and careful hair.

Those bony shoulders and gangly legs
Play football now and not with trains
Hair gel, not conkers by your bed
Ferrous old nails now left in drains.

But when the secret-night comes
Surrounded by innocent treasures
Out peeps the aged blanket, the green bunny
Manhood beckons, but childhood is not yet done.

Praxis

They hardly noticed the first ones. There must have been a first one that was the tiny, disregarded signal of the way things would be but, like most things, it only assumed importance much later, when the impact was so devastating. It would have been funny if it just *so* wasn't.

Kate's story was probably typical. The first one, the very first one, she couldn't clearly remember. Someone must have passed it on to her. She was very young then and didn't have much money so the chance of a couple of hours of free entertainment had been a boon, a way to while away a few spare hours. She remembered the way it had made her feel – her heart hammering, her breath held, every atom focused on it; there was something which drew her in and bound her to it, but it seemed so harmless that she didn't even try and stop it. She had laughed about it with her friends and they had mocked it together, so confident and sure that it wasn't, could never be for the likes of them – only for greyer, older, tinged with failure, *other* people; never for them – with thick, shiny hair that was often tossed about, strong limbs and dazzling teeth – what would they need it for? What could it want with them? But …

Years later, sleepless in the small hours, Kate traced her decline from glossy and dazzling, step by tiny step into grey, formless and failing. The waste of the hours, days, months since that first time seemed to her like a looming slag heap of wishful thinking that was about to slide and obliterate the shape of the life she had expected for herself. The first had led to more and more and each then multiplied. She had sensed others like her nearby on occasion, small clues fanning her belief but she hadn't wanted to admit it, to feel the shame. She knew the only way now was to face it, name it.

She had made contact with the others, stepping softly around the romance section until she was close enough for whispered contact and instructions. They hadn't believed change was possible but slowly their numbers had increased, torn between the shame and the hope that they could recover. Now they met monthly and the Mills and Boon support group was born. Someday they believed they would heal and only read literary fiction.

Christina May

What I write

I write pictures
that hang crookedly
on your wall.
I write ideas
as they leave my arms
through my fingers
onto keys.
Just letters
joined into words
to make sentences
that I twist
and poke
and annul.
What I end up with,
invariably,
is not what I wrote.
It's something else
An end product
arrived at somehow
by the letters
and the words
rearranging
themselves.
I write surprises
that hang crookedly
out of
my mind.

Suttee

By the time we arrive to take our places within the families allotted to us by karma, fate, or The Gods, our parents are used goods. Their complex back stories smolder silently behind the walls of our simple here-and-now worlds, an occasional flicker alerting us to other times, other places and, should the glow be particularly fierce, the other people that they had been. Pre us.

Sometimes it will be a comment that oxygenates the embers, a careless word fizzing like hot cinders across the homestead to burn innocent ears. Or maybe the accidental disinterring of a photograph, a bundle of letters or some other keepsake will conjure secrets that sting for years to come, without anyone explaining why. It is fortunate that most of us just detect the singed memories that our parents keep like an occasional, not quite visible, swirl of smoke.

Of course, the past burns closer when our parents have yet to discover that the small, simple creatures they gave life to will suck in the tiniest details for a sense of the world. Odd sparks of the pre us era are seized upon as irregularities and affix themselves in young minds, melding into something more understandable or amusing. It may take decades for us to know who our parents really are and, at sixty one Herb had ceased much interest in his parents' ancient earlier lives until his childhood home alighted in visitations once again.

Thinking through the smog of time as he stood in his mother's uninhabited home, he was able to identify the first glimmer that things were not quite as regular in this house as in others. It was that afternoon when he'd left the table in a hurry and nearly collided with a brown man in a turban. There *would* have been a collision had the fellow not sunk himself back into the rug from which he'd appeared. If he had stayed there, beneath the floor, he would have been more or less forgotten but a second later he'd sprinted past Herb and disappeared through the closed wardrobe door.

Even so, Herb had had important things on his mind and dismissed this occurrence for later exploration. Ayah was approaching with a scolding tone and he braced himself for the conversation to come. He knew there would be a reaction to what he was about to say there always was a reaction to his thoughts, for unlike his peers with their disinterested English nannies, Herb had been blessed with Ayah and Ayah treated all of his utterances as declarations from The King.

He wanted the *right* reaction and, having watched his older cousins wheedle through tea parties and family picnics, he realised that he was short of a few whining siblings for reinforcement. Hearing the light pad of Ayah's feet approach the nursery, he grabbed a stuffed bear from the bed to act as co-conspirator.

'I don't want to drink milk anymore.' He started the confrontation as soon as she came into view, the bear held up like a sword, 'Teddy hates it, too!'

This deputation was effective in making the brown marbles he'd decided she used for eyes roll up toward her scarf while her lips curved into indulgence. He and Teddy alone were not to be taken seriously. Herb knew that grown up men would always be the best validation of anything and so he breathed in, Teddy now tossed on the bed, and imparted the secret that he'd decided was just for him:

'The man hates milk *so much*, he's hiding in the wardrobe!'

Of course men do not suddenly pop up from nowhere and run across landings to hide in the nearest cupboard, Herb was not stupid. He expected to find the closet empty, should he look, just a dream or a memory from Ayah's tales, but Ayah had come in to chide about the milk and now the man who'd appeared out of air was a very real and, judging by Ayah's face, very disconcerting thing. Her coppery skin had turned to ash and the brown marbles skittered across the widened whites of her eyes.

Herb was about to say that he didn't really mind milk all that much when she squatted down, fingers tight around his arm, and pulled him to the window. Ayah never played with him this way and he squealed in delight at the wrestle, putting his free arm across her throat for a tug of her veil.

A slap on his fingers caused him to check her face again and he patted a hand on her shoulder the way Daddy placated his mother, whispering that it was all right, Teddy really did like to drink milk.

Keeping her hold on his arm, Ayah opened the window and called down to Mali in 'chi chi'.

Herb held his breath for 'in this country it is neither necessary nor desired for any of our household to use anything other than The King's English'. Herb had heard this so often from his father that he knew it by rote and began to wish a beaker of milk would appear so that he could demonstrate a change of heart.

The gardener had never entered the house but this day he came right in and up the stairs, scattering damp soil all along the runner and through to the nursery. Herb started jumping up and down, worried about the mess but excited at this latest new game, until Ayah took him into her own room next door where she raised the heavy lid of her trunk for him to play among her saris. This was perhaps the most unusual occurrence of that afternoon as these brightly coloured billows were forbidden from his tampering hands. Lost in the feel of silks and cotton, his fingers fiddling with inlaid pieces of glass and shining beads, Herb became only slightly aware of Mali's surprised tones through the wall.

Ayah told him later 'Do not speak of these things, it must be our secret. If Wardrobe Man is here again you must not look, you must turn your back'. She turned around to show him her back, 'See? Like this, see? Do as I do.'

She spun round and round in her yellow sari to illustrate what he must do and Herb caught on and whirled himself ever madly until they were both laughing and he became dizzy and had to be laid on the bed.

'You must never acknowledge him,' she said as they went back to see the wardrobe now empty of strangers, 'always pretend that he is not here.'

'That would be rude, Ayah.'

'No, not rude, it is not real person like you and like Ayah. He will not mind, it is just someone else's dream.'

As Herb grew up he was often reminded that blanking a visitor was not quite the done thing, 'no matter how dreary' his father would say. That may have been why he occasionally heard his mother speak to Wardrobe Man. Not with her customary, formal tone used for the important military men who would come on business, but with that soft tenderness reserved for his father when they thought no one could hear. That special voice told Herb that despite Wardrobe Man being an Indian, he was something more than a servant, perhaps it was something to do with what Ayah had explained as 'caste'. Whatever the reason, he was an extraordinary Indian man and he must not be spoken to by Herb.

Once Herb began school, Wardrobe Man melded into the vague mesh of memories of home. He became part of the colonial nik naks brought back to England when they had resettled after the war, of no more prominence than the flowers weaved into his bedside rug or the topees in a corner of the orangery.

He thought little of the man as his childhood passed, presuming that it had been an imagining inspired by his cross-cultural surroundings and the lingering whispers of lives far away. By the time he'd reached eighteen, all the Indian servants had left them and his father, keen to embrace a more modern lifestyle in retirement, called in a designer from London.

This man was quite ruthless and talked a lot about the importance of suggesting light and air. He wanted the windows stripped of their art deco leading and brought swatches of material that Herb's mother refused to see. Rugs were given a final beating to be stored in the attic and the parque was smothered in shag. Animal skins, ivory and antlers were banished and their wooden box of a television replaced by an enormous bright orange globe that transmitted in colour. The house was now in Twentieth Century Britain and while Herb had to agree that there was light and air, his mother seemed swathed in a shadow.

Fortunately, Herb was rarely home as he had taken a job at a record shop while waiting for University to begin. His mind was busy with music and parties and sometimes it was infused with cannabis and occasionally, perhaps Saturdays, something more interesting. There was little time to think of ghosts although in the brief periods that he was at the house, and awake, he noticed that his mother often appeared to be thinking herself somewhere else.

One evening, as he was about to rush to a rendezvous, a documentary about The Beatles came on the great round TV. He'd become a bit of an aficionado and dithered in the doorway, deliberating whether to be late. His mother pointed at the screen and, expecting another complaint about the band's ever-growing hair, he turned to leave.

'India is not the country I knew,' she said.

Always aware she had been born, raised and married in that strange land, Herb now wondered that he had never been curious. Since The Beatles had gone over there it had become very fashionable and he started to quiz her but she waved him away, saying that it was too long ago.

'You had a man friend there, a fellow in a turban,' Herb was surprised at his sudden memory of those odd occasions when a figure would materialise and wander about the house.

'Preposterous, Herbie, we lived in the compounds, had our own English villages. There was no fraternising.'

'He would visit you here, like a dream.'

She sat up straight and stared at her son.

'Used to turn up out of nowhere and mooch about' he continued, enjoying his freedom of speech as a new adult.

'You saw him?' a whisper.

'Oh yes, he was quite a wheeze the way he let himself in and out. I think he frightened Ayah, though.'

'Herbert, there are things you don't know, many things,' she said.

'Tell me, it's fascinating, how did he come and go like that? Even into your bedroom, I'd hear you talking.'

'No, you didn't, Herb, you can't have done.' She stood up and walked to where there used to be a mantel piece, before her husband had the great fireplace boarded up, central heating being the way to go. 'Look, there were some Hindi people who were very spiritual. They believed certain things, strange things, I really can't explain. The power of the subconscious or something. I know who you think you saw but he really wasn't here, not in person.'

'I think Ayah tried to tell me something like that' Herb regretted that he'd touched such a nerve, particularly when he wanted to leave and forget about his folks for the night.

He changed the subject while checking his jacket pocket for wallet and keys. 'You rescued her, didn't you, in India?'

'Rescued?' his mother was still thinking of Wardrobe Man. 'Oh yes, well, it was her mother I helped but it's true that Ayah would have become an orphan had the suttee gone ahead.'

'Suttee? She was going to throw herself on her husband's funeral pyre, really? That's horrid, however did you -'

'Herbie, this was all a long time ago, shouldn't you be somewhere?'

Over the years Herb would attempt conversations about India but his mother remained guarded and his father, never having held much truck with the country, died without imparting anything more than a disparaging grunt. Content with a housekeeper, his mother was happy for her son to move away, marry and lose himself in his own existence. They saw each other at Easter, the young family making it a bit of a tradition to drive down and stay the long weekend, and so for all of his adulthood Herb only saw Wardrobe Man twice. He was not even sure that it was the same chap as the turban had gone, leaving a bald head that reflected his father's Habitat lighting. The second apparition fashioned a greying moustache and this time Herb decided that ghosts, were they possible, would not age in this way. It was far more likely that all the junk they'd brought over from India had something infused that became active in colder climates and caused people in the house to hallucinate.

He was only staying there now because of the neighbours. His mother had been hospitalised for some weeks and the people on the new estate opposite their grounds had complained of squatters. Police had broken in twice to inspect lights going on and off and the sound of parties but nothing had appeared out of turn. It was thought easier for Herb to move in and keep intruders at bay and he did suppose that he ought to be at his mother's side, although she wasn't at all lucid.

Wardrobe Man came and went. His gait was less steady due to a curve in his back but Herb was now certain it was he. At the hospital he would ask his mother about him in the hope that she would be jolted back into the world but what she said was hard to decipher. A doctor suggested it might be Punjabi and arranged for a colleague to try and converse.

'She thinks she is at home,' the helpful interpreter explained, 'and that the hospital staff are her servants. She is most agitated that white people are doing menial jobs and asked me why the sweeper is not an Indian.'

Herb blushed, he knew from Ayah that the sweeper's job had been to empty the latrines.

'She thinks she is a Rajah!' laughed the doctor as he walked away.

Herb made a note on his iPhone to bring in a few things from home, dig out a silk shawl or some beads.

That night as he excavated the contents of a satinwood trunk at the end of her bed, looking for artefacts to take to the ward, he heard her voice. Startled, the lid almost clapped shut on his fingers as he dropped it to hasten to the landing. She was downstairs, he could hear her, talking softly but ever-clearer, she was coming this way. Stretching over the banister, he heard the rustle of a starchy nightdress as she walked through the hallway, her hand around Wardrobe Man's crooked fist. She looked just as he had left her two hours before, hair brushed tidily away from her face and cannula taped to her hand.

'Mother!' he called, 'how did you get here?'

Neither of them looked up to acknowledge him and so he hung there, silent, head stretching as far as it would with his feet on the floor. The banister was mahogany and many years of polish had made it slippery.

As the figures went into the drawing room he steadied himself and laughed. 'She could have taught The Beatles a thing or two about teleportation.' He thought, 'My God, no wonder she thinks she's at home, she is!'

'Herbert, are all these lights necessary?'

He was left in darkness as the landing light clicked off.

During the next few days the nurses reported that their patient seemed further away, talking less and rarely opening her eyes. Herb knew that they were suggesting deterioration but he somehow couldn't feel it. While she may not be here mentally in this clankety bed with its metal railings and that horrid smell of hospital, he knew that her mind remained very active elsewhere.

Some evenings after kissing her sleeping cheek on the ward, he'd let himself into the house and find her there alone. On others he'd see or hear them together. Wardrobe Man no longer walked, he would be supine on a chaise or the floor. He wore night clothes and appeared once with a tube up his nose. Herb kept his distance from these apparitions, not out of fear but to allow them their time together.

During the day when he was at the hospital and his mother perfectly still, he would smile at the thought that the best way to visit her really would be to stay at home and see her fading in and out at will.

One morning he decided to do just that although it wasn't she he was most concerned about, it was Wardrobe Man. The fellow had been flickering in and out of Herb's vision throughout the night. While previously his presence had looked solid, now there was something more ethereal as though he couldn't quite make himself stay. This new kind of coming and going, sometimes every second and other times less frequent, was disturbing. It was more than the apparent difficulty in transporting that concerned Herb, it was Wardrobe Man's appearance. His eyes were unfocused and mouth mucoid and twisted. Herb could tell by the heave of his wasted chest that things were not good.

He was also worried that his mother may turn up and be distressed by this ailing but as it happened, when she did materialise right next to where Wardrobe Man lay on the living room floor, she calmly took her friend's head in her lap and stroked his face smooth. Herb saw their eyes meet as Wardrobe Man convulsed for a second before disappearing once again.

For a good few minutes she just sat there, expressionless, and then she began to tremble. Herb went to her, arms ready to embrace but there was no acknowledgement that she could see him and so he froze as he watched her gradually master the use of her legs to stand, swaying.

Keeping an arm out ready in case of a fall, Herb smelt her carbolic soap as she moved just inches past him, eyes fixed on the wall where the fireplace once stood.

'Mother,' he said, as she dissolved into the Anaglypta.

About twenty minutes later Herb's phone bleeped.

'Please come to the hospital as soon as you can, someone will be waiting at the main reception.'

That drive to the hospital was one that Herb had mentally rehearsed. It was as he had expected, a momentous and grave journey and yet, fogged by his disturbed night and tendered by what he'd just witnessed, there was a tranquility as he traveled toward the inevitable.

He wasn't perturbed by the fire engines or police vehicles near the ambulance bays, presuming a drill or false alarm, but when he stepped into the main foyer the ward sister was waiting with a hospital manager.

They explained that the ward had been cordoned off. They took him into a visitor's room. It had to be opened with a key. There was a box of tissues on a table. Some comfortable chairs. A picture of clouds on the wall. Leaflets about bereavement.

'I'd like to see her.' Herb hadn't had to ask why he was here.

'That isn't actually possible,' said the manager, holding a hand toward a chair.

The ward sister started to cry, words blundering between her sobs: 'Just went up, a ball of flame, death instantaneous, she won't have known a thing, never made a sound, we don't know how it happened, nothing else was touched, not even the oxygen by the bed, the fire brigade are all over it, the police are taking everybody's statements, someone said it was spontaneous combustion. Oh, I am so terribly sorry I really don't know what to say!'

A fire investigator came in and introduced himself. Something was said about Herb taking some time and providing a statement later. An investigation had been started, a report would be made.

Herb nodded, turned to thank them all and stood up to leave. He was greeted at the door by the hospital chaplain. There was an invitation to have some words, perhaps use the chapel.

'I am not sure that your lot can help me,' said Herb, and a chair was shoved behind him as his legs gave way.

The sister remembered her training and ran into the corridor, muttering about blood sugar and a glass of milk.

Herb could only elicit noises: 'Sut – sut – sut-'

The chaplain laid a hand upon his shoulder and the other men took their leave. After a few minutes the nurse reappeared, holding forth a glass of milk as though it were the elixir of life.

Lunging out of the chair, Herb knocked the glass from her and in this new world where everything was happening in slow motion he saw its white liquid momentarily suspended in the air like ectoplasm.

He continued to gasp: 'Sut-sut-sut- she committed suttee!

The Umbilicus

It happened on a Sunday. It was because it happened on a Sunday that I remember. Nothing happened on a Sunday, ever. There were occurrences, certainly, and routines, but nothing actually happened on a Sunday. Our parents saw to that.

Nobody said it was never to be mentioned, I just knew. Life was like that for children back then and I suppose this lead to everything sort of coalescing in our heads. Because I was not to speak of it, perhaps it became condensed in my conscience into something it wasn't it was always hard to tell. I would pick it out from whichever part of my maturing mind it was meshed, usually at night while Clara lay mercifully mute.

Over the years I suppose the memory changed, taking on new life, evolving with the new found nubs of knowledge which I mostly collected from factory girls on the bus. I say 'knowledge' but of course I would later find that most of their chatter of the fellows they were courting was nonsense. I loved to listen, though, and not just to their tales. I loves their voices, harsh and grating like the sound of the rooks in our garden. And I loved their words, the funny little phrases each assembled that were alien and yet the Queen's English all the same.

Around the time I started my menses, the memory of that Sunday started to ferment quite feverishly. Once or twice I coughed or let my pillow thunk to the lino, just to wake Clara, not wanting to be alone with its new reality. I tested the water a bit with vague references but she would give me that scornful big sister stare, the one that suggested there were sixteen years between us when in fact it was just sixteen minutes. The look that said she did not know what I was talking about, that no one could know what I was talking about and how my head was full of silliness that my mouth ought to know not to speak.

I had been born with a handicap, you see, that was what they called it back then. Twins often were. They said I was defective because it had taken me longer to learn how to speak and I was later found to be a little deaf. While walking had come naturally to Clara, I would shuffle and eventually crawl to keep up and if ever I complained, my parents would explain how I was a very lucky little girl not to have been born dead.

A glass of bucks fizz on our twenty first birthday broke my silence. It was our party, our parents had hired the town hall and Mother had even managed to secure the latest swing band from the city, ensuring that it was all rather grand. Clara was surrounded by her pretty friends in their circle skirts, some erstwhile suitors hovering. I shuffled self-consciously through Clara's throng, my kitten heels and harsh crinoline making me awkward.

'Little Sister,' she pealed. Those sixteen minutes between our first furious breaths and I was forever diminished, affixed by time to my station.

'Come outside,' I said. Tonight I would be brave.

She looked perplexed and shrugged an exaggerated apology to her friends, as if to say 'you know what she's like.' I was used to that.

I took her by the hand, childish gestures remaining between us like the umbilicus that had almost killed me. The champagne in her blood made her follow.

We nodded and smiled at our well-wishers on our way to the door and escaped before Mother could notice. I lost my shoe on the steps leading down from the entrance and a ladder shot straight up one nylon. Clara laughed and gave her usual loud cries of despair for my lack of polish but my look told her that tonight would be different and she suddenly went solemn. Perhaps she had guessed what was to come.

So we stood there, and I asked her. I ask her for the first time in fifteen years. I said it. I took it out and let it exist there in the air we shared, our faces a mirrored cameo in the moonlight.

'You weren't there,' was her response.

Not 'I don't remember', not 'it didn't happen'. *You were not there.*

Then she whirled her skirt and went back up the steps to our guests while I stood, on one stupid foot, unable to move. This was the most confirmation Clara could have conceded.

It had been customary long before our coming of age for Clara to claim that I was stealing her memories. Being the eldest, whatever happened, happened to her. My presence or participation would have been mere coincidence and, as happenings became more grown up, an inconvenience. This retort was the nearest she had come to agreeing that it *had* happened, her claim that I was not there more validating than had she said I was mad. It had happened and now I knew for sure that it had happened to me.

Once it was out, albeit not actually spoken of but confided by allusion, my head felt roomier. I lay more easily in my bed, less anxious about the thing in Korea, unperturbed by borrowed hat pins, less fretful of Clara's late hours and our parents' scolds. I had been set free, *she* had set me free. Until I had twins of my own.

It was my husband who noticed. He even found a book about it in the library: *The Hysterical Female.* I was given pills and they made me hysterical.

We were about fifty years of age when I broached the subject again. It was late one afternoon while Clara and I were alone in my kitchen. The sun was low and shooting straight onto my silver.

'That Sunday.'

'Best forgotten,' she said.

'I can't forget.'

'It didn't happen.'

What didn't happen, Clara?'

This put her on the spot. She fiddled with the beads on her neck and stared into the distance, her eyes seeing something she wasn't going to share.

Of course she was right and I knew I had to be careful because not long before this attempt I had seen a doctor about my monthlies and he'd told me of a mysterious new illness, scratching it out on a bit of paper for me: False Memory Something Or Other. So I was afraid. Not afraid that I had it, afraid it had afflicted Clara. One neurotic was enough for our parents I could not give them two.

So it happened on a Sunday. Eighty five years ago, thereabouts. Oh, I haven't been mulling it all this time, no, I had family commitments and a little job at the library to keep my mind busy. Then as we grew old and suffered our cerebral vascular attacks, both Clara and I had to start to be careful about our wearing cognition.

The thing is, today she said something. All of a sudden. Out of the blue. With it being Sunday, there's not much for us to do in here, The Activities Woman only works in the week, so perhaps Clara had been thinking.

'That Sunday,' she said.

'Yes.'

'Did it happen?'

'Yes.'

'I was thinking I may have been mistaken –'

I took her by the hand and said 'Best forgotten.'

'I wanted to protect you.'

'Oh, Clara, you did! Mother said she'd never seen a man run so fast.'

Kelly Mpacko

What I write

Prose, never poetry (though I try to be poetic). Mainly sad, creepy or down-right depressing. It is, at least in my hands, impossible to write something cheery without resorting to cliché. The dark is much easier to embellish. While scribblings of a novel remain resolutely buried within the mechanics of my hard-drive, my writing has become more diminutive recently. The arrival of two small people in my home over the last few years has made my stories shorter and shorter. Flash fiction is a fun and welcoming format for those pressed for time. The novel will just have to wait.

Pitter-Patter

Bare feet on floor boards. That's what I can hear. Only we put down carpet the week we moved in. The modern minimalism of polished wood is lost on people who feel even the slightest of drafts penetrate their bones. I lie on the bed listening, my hand unconsciously rubbing my swollen belly. The sound, running feet, is coming from the next room and has woken me every night since we moved in. The room is full of boxes; no space for running. The baby must be able to hear it too. She is kicking in time with the steps.

The decoration of the nursery has not uncovered any obvious source. We have even brought in pest control to help with the search. Squirrels in the loft space? Rats in the basement? Nothing. Still the noise continues. Everyone has a theory: the central heating wafting; the house 'settling', timbers contracting; wind blowing across the chimney pots and even the vibrations from a passing car's stereo can, apparently, make the walls hum. On top of all that, there is always the possibility that my hormones have heightened my senses. Apparently. He doesn't hear it, and he is right next to me.

Newborn at my breast, I hear it again. The same pattern repeats. Baby wriggles in response, liquid leaking down her chin and washing over my goose bumps. The sickly sweet stench of this, my own milk, nauseates me as I try to calm her. She rolls her eyes clumsily, as newborns do, but this ordinary movement suddenly looks so extraordinary. She does not latch back on until the noise has ceased. The regained rhythm partially pacifies both of us. My heart begins to slow. I am convinced that the footsteps have become louder, but he still does not hear them.

Turquoise eyes stare back at me. She blinks furiously and we laugh hysterically at the ludicrousness of the game. She runs to hide in the same place again. I pretend to look for her again. A year has been and gone, yet the footsteps continue. They seem to get stronger every month. I know I am not mad: she reacts to the strange noises too. Her shoulders shudder and legs spasm and I can only watch in horror. As soon as they stop, the writhing stops. She recovers. She smiles. She laughs. We play. I know I am not mad.

I lie in bed, the pillow damp under my cheek. My hand reaches behind me to feel his warmth, for comfort, for forgiveness. I replay the image in my head. *Turquoise eyes stare back at me, unblinking. The carpet mottles with her blood.* I close my eyes forcing more tears to drip. Suddenly, the footsteps begin and get louder. They are coming this way. I sit up with a start and stare at the open door. She decelerates as she enters the room: pitter-patter, pitter-patter until she is at the end of the bed. Turquoise eyes stare back at me.

Alex McHugh

What I write

What I write is jokes but they're not very funny. They certainly haven't made any one laugh yet. But that's what I want, people throwing their heads back, howling with laughter. That's all I've ever wanted. Words on paper, in the right order, in the right language - bang! - everybody laughing. That's the dream.

So far there's been short stories, usually involving self-styled aesthetes labouring in down at heel shopping centres, or lonely souls getting lost on windswept hills, or kleptomaniac medical students getting themselves caught with bloodied red hands.

Ha ha ha. Ha!

She Is

I don't mean to be cruel but the two of them couldn't have looked more like men if they'd tried. They hadn't of course, tried. In fact, they'd done everything possible to pass themselves off as women - respectable women who drank Prosecco in M&S dresses.

Their wigs had slipped. They had five o'clock shadows and hairy wrists. To compliment the gossip and cackles they had bobbing Adam's apples and broad shaking shoulders. Their immense jaw lines, boulder-like and unmistakably male, were by the by.

Later, when I approach with the PDQ machine and ask 'Who's paying?' they answer, with smiles, in unison: 'She is.'

Sending and Receiving

Let's get this thing out and pinned to a cork. Stop it going anywhere, for one thing, and if it's not beautiful then it's unusual at least, and worthy of peoples' attention. Look, I'll transmit it to you as best as I can, you do the pinning. On to that cork, or whatever software you have. Or just pin it into your mind's eye, if that's not too distressing an image. As far as I understand the situation I'll be sending this thing out to you via a series of rhythmic pulsations, or waves, or possibly in some way I'm not yet conscious of being capable of. Might do you well to consider how certain creatures call out into darkened forests, looking for lovers. Shimmering scales, whispering lips, moonlit vibrations in clefts and pools, that kind of thing. There's a myriad of desperate messages wefting and warping over black branches. Pheromones in the dark is perhaps what I'm hinting at here. But listen, if you can pick this one thing out through the stink of everything else, however it comes to you, just stick it down somewhere, would you? I can't myself. I'm indisposed. I might even be dead. All I can do for now is lie here and attempt to transmit this thing. By thing I mean story, and by story I'm obviously referring to myself. I'm the story. The desperate messages are solely concerned with myself myself and how it was I got myself in love and how it was I got myself struck through the stomach with a silver lance, all of which follows on from the great unfurling of my, the awakening of my, perhaps the teasing out of my, that is to say ... hummmmmm. Shimmer shimmer. Whisper whisper. Weft. Warp. Pin.

The Old School On Top Of The Hill

Anyone who made it to the top of the tallest, most brutal of the hills just south of the city would find as their reward an ancient building made of stone. It had been a monastery, and more recently a school. Paint peeled from the walls these days and some of the doors hung precariously on one hinge, still, it was not unusual for it to attract many visitors, although at this precise moment that was a near impossibility. Like the hill on which it stood, and the city it overlooked, and indeed a great many parts of the region, this ancient and impressive building had for many days been almost completely hidden under deep snow.

Olive, in her long black coat - which was beautiful, though perhaps not entirely suitable - was happily marching up the path towards the top of the hill, crunching the snow with her big black boots because that was the way to do it. Either side of her the snow rose to smoothly cover the hedges. The branches of the trees beyond were layered thick, so thick she'd sometimes hear one snapping off somewhere further up the path, or back down below her. Occasionally she passed small dilapidated buildings where the snow came up to the windows and lay heavy on the roof just above. There were bits of crumbling wall too, and the odd unintelligible road sign and, once, she saw in a clearing at a bend in the path, an old abandoned cart with a broken wheel. Here she paused to gently press her fingers into a snow-lined spoke. It was a sad old thing, stuck there like that with no hope escape. Olive preferred to imagine it in its heyday, filled with old-world sacks of apples or barrels of wine. When two small birds suddenly appeared, dipping and twittering around over her head, she briefly cast herself as some quaint character from an old-fashioned novel, saying aloud and in an appropriate accent: 'and then, after breakfast, dressed in her clogs and bonnet, she climbed the ten mile hill from Pont-l'Eveque to Kingdom Come.' She flicked the wet from her fingers and laughed, with her breath everywhere and her cheeks stinging.

Onwards, upwards. Onwards and upwards. That was the way, was the way, was the way.

The higher she climbed, the more of the city she saw spreading out beneath her, although it was really more of a town, an old medieval type, and of course she could barely see it at all, so thoroughly had it been covered by the snow. Holding on to two black saplings at the side of the path, with her head poked between them and her eyes narrowed, she could pick out not much more than the almost vanished outlines of some of the larger buildings, the odd streak of cleared road, a floating stretch of telephone wire, but less and less of these things the further she climbed. Onwards, upwards, onwards and upwards.

Tony O'Neill

What I write

What I write is rubbish poetry. No, it really is. Please don't read any of my poems in this collection, as they're poor. Not very good at all. Doggerel at best. I think I once strung together three or four lines in succession that were okay, but you'd have to buy a previous anthology to find them: *Words from Nowhere,* I think. Or perhaps *Out of Our Minds.* Can't even remember what poem it was, something about a fish...maybe...can't remember. Anyway, since then it's all been dross, and continues to be so. Downhill all the way. Especially since the operation.

79

NO FUTURE!!
Neatly embroidered and correctly spelt,
Complete with exclamation marks, tidily defiant
On his jeans,
Adeptly slashed then stitched to prevent unwanted
Fraying. Diffident he sits in his corner of the bus
Hoping to catch everyone's attention, nobody's eye.
Childwall Punk.
But the next stop brings the inevitable drunk and the drunk,
Of course, sits next to Childwall Punk and says,
"A'right, kid, are you a punk?"
And Childwall Punk says, "Yeh," but in a small faraway
Voice.
"Yerwha'?" says the drunk
And Childwall Punk say, "Yes,"
But louder now so other people hear and turn
Imperceptibly,
Ostensibly engrossed in their e-lectronic books
But inwardly thanking their own god of luck that Punk
Has saved them from Childwall Drunk.
"I was a punk," says Childwall Drunk, "when punks were really punks.
Gobbed on Sid Vicious once; he didn't seem to mind.
Every Saturday night me and me bird pogoing
Round Eric's in a shower of phlegm. Happy days…
Then we pogoed into marriage but it all fell apart when she left me
For some New Romantic tosser. Chemistry teacher."

Then he leans close to Punk Boy and he holds out a hand
That trembles with the weight of his life;
And Punk Boy recoils,
As politely as he can, from the smack of the whisky sour stench.
But the drunk leans closer still until his purple glistening lips
Are pressed against the ear
Of the trembling little lost boy of a punk.

And his mouth opens wide, as if about to yawn from the weariness
Of all the world upon him. But no yawn comes,
Just an animalistic groan as his stomach empties out
In a cataract of biblical proportions.
The e-book devotees abandon all pretence, shrinking
Backwards to avoid the brutal gush
Which envelops Childwall Punk Boy and decorates his head
Like the topping on some grotesque ice-cream cone.

Sluiced out inside the man gets grandly to his feet,
Sweeps his arm towards the sobbing, stinking boy
And proclaims to all the bus, "I may be very drunk,
But that my friends, is what I *call* a punk!"

Not So Famous Albanians

Q: Who was the last king of Albania?
A: King Zog

I

Curate Zeg was assiduous
In administering to his people,
Always there with a joke and a prayer
While collecting for the new church steeple;
But while his smile and holy ways
Were winning parishioners' hearts,
He was siphoning off church funds to Spain;
He was only good in parts.

II

Postman Znock was young and flighty;
Many a spinster in floral nightie
Waited each morning, unloved and lonely,
Believing him her One and Only,
Stood by the letterbox, trembling and quivery
For a Postman Znock Special Delivery.

III

Doctor Zordas was a stickler
When treating Albania's sick:
If they didn't get well through traditional means
He'd beat them with a stick.
Drastic illnesses, drastic cures
Was the doctor's stock-in-trade,
He'd flog them with relish at the drop of a hat -
Doctor Zordas must be obeyed.

IV

Housemaid Znee worked hard to survive,
Up every morning at the stroke of five,
Running hot water for Milady's bath,
Cleaning up dog muck from the garden path,
Scraping out the grate of last night's ashes,
Fetching fresh wax for the Master's moustaches,
Until aged thirty-nine in a mid-life crisis
She changed her name to *Prepatellar Bursitis.*

More Not So Famous Albanians

I

Captain Zlog, brave and fierce,
Careening around the univierce
In his bold, unhygienic interplanetary quest,
Wearing dirty old undies and unsanitary vest:
He's no hot water, the boiler went kaput
When Starship Tirana hit an old Russian sput
Nick, now he's searching for the planet where the Zargons dwell –
They've very poor eyesight and no sense of smell.

II

Baker Zdozen was numerically challenged
And thought thirteens was twelves;
No matter how often he'd count out his bread
There were too many loaves on his shelves.
The townsfolk showed no sympathy
And got up a lengthy petition
To replace the poor sod with someone new -
Now their baker's an arithmetician.

III

Shepherd Zpy was fond of sheep
(But not in the biblical sense),
He loved to count them to get to sleep
As they leapt o'er hedgerow and fence;
But as he slumbered one summer's day
He was woke by a strident shout
From the farmer next door*, purple with rage
Who told him to get the flock out.

*Farmer Zdorta

IV

Mother Zruin, the convent head,
Alone at night in her convent bed,
Praying for her sisters to be free of sin,
Slowly knocking back the convent gin,
Praying for the pauper, the beggar and the gipsy,
The more she prayed the more she felt tipsy,
Praying for the rich folk and praying for the poor,
And praying Father Zappa would come tapping on her door…

chien dormant au musée d'art moderne

One holiday,
Escaping the rain in some middling French town
Beside the sea,
I slunk into the grandly named Musée d'Art Moderne
To pass the time and take some
Arty tea.
When it comes to modern art I don't know very much
But I do, sure as eggs, know what I like:
Give me pictures with people in that tell a proper tale
Like that parasol woman on a bike.

Well, this gallery in Drizzlyville was much like all the others
With the cloying smell of beeswax in the air,
A despondent attendant fetching bogeys from his nose
That he'd deftly wipe off beneath his chair.
So,
Sidling past the portraits of pointy-faced people
And sculptures decidedly risqué
And nameless shapeless things made from rusty old tin cans
I finally found the sign that said: CAFÉ.

The arrows led me on through several rooms more,
Some Picassos, an early work of Pollock's,
Almost blank canvases with random gobs of paint
And some more modern sculptures that were not very good.
Explanations on the walls spoke of "Gestural Painting,"
Of "Abstraction" and "Creative Dynamics,"
But the thing that caught my eye was a small mongrel dog,
Asleep beneath some Vorticist ceramics.

I gave closer inspection to make sure it was alive
And not some clever clockwork-driven children's toy
Or a 3-D picture painted flush upon the floor
That the arty folk I know would call tromp loy.
But a dog it was, its smell worse than its bite,
Rhythmically growling as it snored,
Its spasmodic dreamy twitches ignored by the attendant
Slouching gallicly impassive, and bored.
The room itself was empty save for Fido and me
And this attendant, the empty headed fool,
So I girded loins and walked over to the man,
Dusting off the little French I'd learned at school:
"Excusez-moi," I pointed, "un chien dans la salle,
Removez-le, monsieur, s'il vous plait."
Then I did some franglais gestures like that shoulder thing they do,
And said BOF! in a chummy kind of way.
He gave a sideways look, profound in its contempt,
Muttered something that ended in, "Alors!"
Then went back to his dreams of abstract naked ladies
While I returned to Fido on the floor.

But then a thought struck me like a slap in *le visage,*
Which made me stop and do a sudden turn:
"Ce chien smellie qui est dormant sous les vases,
Il n'est pas une pièce de votre art moderne…?"
With indolence so practised that it must have taken years
The Frenchman handed me a leaflet (en anglais),

Which praised *Le chien dormant* as a work of great perception
By the famous Belgian artist Jacques Triché.
A work, it went on, which explores Man's inner soul
Through the medium of dog upon a floor,
By presenting us this mongrel as it sleeps its life away
The artist helps us to explore our inner core…
This twaddle waddled on for several pages more,
In German, French, Spanish and Italian;
But I finally gave it up and passed the leaflet back
When it droned on about his masterpiece, *The Stallion.*

Less artfully than I'd planned I stomped from the room
In search of this elusive café:
To complete a perfect afternoon just as I arrived
They were putting up the sign that said: FERMĒ.
In anger and frustration I made my way outside,
To have a surreptitious little cry,
And I resolved there and then I'd had my fill of Art –
In future, I'll let sleeping dogs lie.

Christmas Without Angels

One Sunday I said
To my wife,
"Have you noticed there are no angels this Christmas?"
"What do you mean?" she said.
"This Christmas," I said,
"Have you noticed there are no angels?"
"No *angels?*" she said.
"No. Have *you* seen any angels?" I said.
"Can't say that I've noticed," she said.
And then we had some tea.

Some days later my wife said
To me,
"I see what you mean."
"What do you mean?" I said.
"About the angels," she said.
"Oh," I said.
"I haven't seen any either:
Not on a Christmas card,
Not on a tree,
None in the papers,
None on TV…
I've looked.
Hard."

We fell silent,
Contemplating Christmas without angels.

Then a single light bulb appeared over two heads
And in a twinkling
We were in the loft,
Opening up our
Big Box of Christmas Stuff.
But
Our cardboard-top-of-the-tree made-by-our-five-year-old-son-twenty-years-ago
Angel, was gone.

We rang the local radio station,
Tony Snell. Breakfast Show,
And our angels were a throwaway item
Just before the sport.
By lunchtime it was proper in the news.
Nobody in Liverpool, it seems,
Had seen an angel this Christmas:
Nobody in Liverpool, it seems,
Had noticed they'd not noticed any angels until we noticed it.

By evening it was regional, on TV:
No Angels in northern England.

Next day,
Those nice, smiley people were reviewing
The papers on Breakfast TV.
The Times said:
MYSTERY OF MISSING ANGELS
The Daily Express said:
ANGEL DROUGHT HITS BRITAIN
The Daily Mail said:
IMMIGRANTS TAKE OUR ANGELS.

All over the country, strange things
Began to happen.
Newcastle lost its Angel of the North,
Monopoly boards across the land
Lost a square in Islington
And poor people, for dessert, just had Delight.
Wide-eyed, gap-toothed schoolchildren,
Earmarked for the part of angels
In a thousand Nativity plays,
Stayed cowering in their beds.

Elsewhere, too, there was panic.
Mrs Merkel, boss of Germany, couldn't locate her first name.
In Venezuela, people went carackers
As the Angel Falls became a trickle.
Los Angeles briefly rioted
Before disappearing from the map.
Angel cakes disappeared from menus,
Even in the best hotels.

So the whole world over
Christmas was ruined.
And although no wars

Stopped and there were no Christmas football games,
Everyone agreed
That a world without angels
Was a world without joy.

On the credit side, that bloody Robbie Williams song was never heard again…

Don't Ask Me

Don't ask me to write you a love poem,
It's not what I do.
I'll do poems that are funny or clever,
A quirky verse or two;
I could knock out a sonnet on drinking too much,
Or how our kids have grown tall:
But don't ask me to write you a love poem,
That's not what I do, at all.
I could churn you out doggerel 'til the dogs come home
Pursued by proverbial cows,
I could turn out some verse on next door's cat
Who sits on our step and meows,
If you want sentimental I'll write dewy-eyed
About Dad's hard life as a docker:
But forget about getting a love poem,
That stuff's not in my locker.
If it's love poems you crave I'll buy you a book
Full of poets who've mastered the art
Of scratching on paper a jumble of words
To melt a coy mistress's heart;
Who'll swoon and sigh from one line to the next,
Who'll weep at the drop of a hat:
But *I'll* not master the love poem,
I can't get my head around that.

The Valentine Card I'll send you each year
With its hackneyed, factory verse
Is the nearest you'll get to a love poem from me
This side of a ride in a hearse.
I've tried to write you a Mills & Boon,
Abandoned more than a few:
So I'll never write you that love poem,
But I love you, my darling, I do.

Mrs Santa Gets A Cob On

Mrs Santa, poor woman, was not a great looker,
Was quick to anger, when the mood took her
(Then Santa would slope away, muttering "Fuck 'er"
And hide in Rudolph's shed).
Our story begins some years ago
When the world was white with chocolate box snow,
The day before Christmas and all set to go,
But Santa was still in his bed.
"Get up, you fat bastard!" cried Mrs Claus,
"You know the Australians are up early doors – "
Then she sniffed, before leaving an ominous pause:
"Have you been out on the ale?
This room stinks like a brewery dog
And you there snoring, you drunken old hog,
Stuck in your pit like a big slobby log
Or a bloody enormous beached whale!
Get out of bed and get your round started
Or millions of kids will wake up broken hearted…"
Santa just belched and then burped and then farted
And sicked a bit onto his sheet.
She pulled off the duvet, grabbed hold of his leg,
"Get up and get moving, I'm not gonna beg,

I've made you some bacon and scrambled egg,
You'll feel better with something to eat."

The very thought of breakfast made Santa turn green,
He didn't dare tell her just where he'd been -
Up half the night drinking turnip poteen
With some leprechauns up from Strabane.
"To be honest, m'dear, I've a real dicky tum,
And I slipped on some ice and bruised all me bum,
My tongue's a bit fuzzy, I feel strangely numb -
I couldn't face any scran.
Just let me roll over for ten minutes more
And then I'll be up and out of the door,
A superfit Santa, as good as before
And away with my big bag of toys."

But alas and alack after all that boozing,
He was dead to the world, monumentally snoozing,
While Mrs Santa was rapidly losing
Her feminine charm and poise –
She stormed from the room in a furious state,
That smelly old pisshead had left it too late,
The reindeer were restless, fed up with the wait:
Things were much worse than she'd feared,
So she stripped off her apron and delved in the cupboard
To dress up like Santa, all padded and blubbered,
She cried to the reindeer, "Onward and up'ard!"
As she deftly slipped on a false beard.
The reindeer responded and up went the sleigh,
Up to the stars, she was on her way,
Mrs Santa F Claus would carry the day -
Then batter him when she got back.
She whizzed round the world at the speed of light,
Dressed up as her husband, the selfish old shite,
By the time she stopped for a drink and a bite
She'd more than half emptied the sack.

Through wind and through rain the brave woman flew,
From Chile to China, from Perth to Peru
And all the while plotting the things that she'd do
To that drunkard husband of hers.
The reindeer, meanwhile, were all pretty shrewd
And kept their heads down, as they sensed her black mood,
They jingled along, subservient, subdued
As if they were saying their prayers.

She got rid of her toys as pink dawn was showing,
Christmas Day had arrived, it was peacefully snowing;
She hadn't done very much ho-ho-hoing,
But she'd finished the job on time.
Still trembling with anger, but also quite knackered
She said to her fellah, "By Jove, I'm cream crackered,
That's the *only* reason you've not been attackèd:
Now get me a gin & lime."
So Santa, now showered, sober and meek,
And vowing to give up the drink (for a week)
Crept up to give her a peck on the cheek
Then went off to mix her a gin.
By the time he returned she was deeply a-snooze,
(Nodded off while watching the news)
So he tenderly slipped off her snow-sodden shoes,
Fetched a blanket and tucked her in.

Well that selfish old Santa had caused a close call,
But on Christmas Day there were presents for all,
Mrs Santa completed her round the world flight
So that parents were woken by shrieks of delight…
Could it happen again? No, there's no cause to fear
Because the very same thing happens EVERY YEAR!

Swimming with Dolphins

Perhaps it's mildly morbid,
This little list I keep,
It makes some people shake their heads,
It makes my loved ones weep;
Although it's slightly tasteless
I'll share my list with you:
It's all the things, before I die, I can't be arsed to do.
It's my Fuck It list, my Sod It list, my Couldn't Give a Toss,
Can't Be Bothered, What's the Point, It's Really No Great Loss;
My list of stuff that willingly I'll die not having done,
A catalogue of crazy stunts that, really, are no fun.

Thrashing round with dolphins,
I'll confidently say,
Is not a thing I'll do before
My expiration day.
No urge to jump off towers
Dangling from a rope,
Don't want to meet a Beatle or audience with the Pope.
It's my Fuck It list, my Sod It list, my Couldn't Give a Toss,
Can't Be Bothered, What's the Point, It's Really No Great Loss.

When I'm well into my dotage,
Frail and nearly blind,
Floating in a balloon
Will be the last thing on my mind.
I'm sure the Queen won't miss me
If I don't dine at the Palace,
And you can shove your Northern Lights up your Aurora Borealace.
It's my Fuck It list, my Sod It list, my Couldn't Give a Toss,
Can't Be Bothered, What's the Point, It's Really No Great Loss.

When I'm getting to the end,
Thin and deathly pale,
I won't shed any tears
If I've never seen a whale,
And as I utter my last words,
Leaving just skin and bones,
Bet your life those words won't be *I never saw the Stones...*
It's my Fuck It list, my Sod It list, my Couldn't Give a Toss,
Can't Be Bothered, What's the Point, It's Really No Great Loss.

When folk gather at my funeral
To look back on my days,
They'll say I was a decent sort
Despite my funny ways,
Then once they've all grown tired
Of the sympathetic bit
They'll mutter as they leave, *He was an apathetic git.*

It's my Fuck It list, my Sod It list, my Couldn't Give a Toss,
Can't Be Bothered, What's the Point, It's Really No Great Loss.
But when my family stand around my grave and gently grieve,
They'll be proud of all the things in life I never did achieve.

Wedded Bliss

In separate rooms they watch TV,

Separate programmes, he and she,

Soaps for one, cars the other,

Sherlock Holmes never meets Big Brother.

Singly anticipating what's on next

Through a self-regulated TV week;

Why bother to share a room and speak

When you can send a friendly text?

Night upon night repeats like this,

They meet on the stair, they share a kiss

And it works for them, this wedded bliss.

A J Taylor

What I write

Write, just write
My inner voice is nagging
Revise, cut, rework
As editor I am scathing
A satisfying sentence
My left brain must be working
Another check tomorrow
To see if it's worth saving.

Bankside (A novel)

Chapter 1 – 1947

After a couple of weeks asking for a job in every place he could think of, Vincent was about to give up. It was a wet Thursday lunchtime when he overheard Miss Barton, one of his teachers, complaining about her greengrocer brother. Apparently, he'd sacked his Saturday assistant leaving himself high and dry.

'If he thinks I'm going to help him on the market on my day off, he can think again,' Miss Barton said. 'I worked on the market every weekend and holiday when I was at teacher training college and I'm not going back now. It's his own fault, he shouldn't be so bad tempered.'

Vincent called at the market after school that same day; it was almost half past four and there were few customers – stragglers looking for bargains. It didn't take long to find, 'Barton's Quality Produce' because it was one of the larger greengrocers on the market and the name was painted on a board that hung at the back of the stall. The board was grimy around the edges and the lettering had begun to fade, the B had almost disappeared. Vincent had asked about a job there two weeks earlier, but had received the familiar rejection.

Some stallholders had already packed up and Barton's didn't have much produce left, a few cabbages, potatoes covered in red soil, and some tired fruit ignored by the shoppers. A middle-aged, overweight man was stacking boxes at one end. Vincent went over to him.

'Excuse me.'

The man looked up.

'I wondered if you needed any help on Saturdays.'

'What sort of help?' The man continued stacking the boxes.

'Help on the stall, anything really. I'm looking for a part time job.'

'I see.' He studied Vincent, put down the box he was holding and pointed to the side of the stall. 'Go and wait over there until I've finished sorting this lot out.'

After he'd packed away the potatoes, the man pushed back his lank, greying hair and beckoned Vincent to join him behind the stall.

'Now then young man. Where do you live, what school do you go to, oh and what's your name?' Barton asked.

'Vincent Duckworth, 25 Shaw Street, I go to St Patrick's.'

'What do you know about fruit and veg'?'

'Not very much, but I can learn quickly.

They eyed each other up.

'Well at least you don't try and make things up - if you had done, I'd have run you off this market as a charlatan.'

Vincent looked at Barton, wondering what he meant.

'Take your jacket off and then put that lot into the rubbish bin,' Barton pointed to a pile of vegetable trimmings. Vincent cringed at his fingernails edged in black. 'We'll see how you get on. The brush and shovel are by the coats.'

Vincent hooked his jacket on a nail at the back of the stall next to a stiff woollen overcoat and, picking up a long brush with stumpy bristles, he swept the debris towards a metal bin that was already half filled with rubbish. He looked around the stall as he swept. Other greengrocers created smart displays, covering their tables with green baize, arranging the fruit in Technicolor pyramids, using fancy script for the price tickets. It looked as though Barton simply tipped his stock into cardboard boxes that rested on the bare boards of trestle tables. Prices were scrawled in crayon on the flap of each box. Even to Vincent's untrained eye, the fruit that was left at the end of the day looked old.

'What's one and eight times three?' Barton asked when Vincent had dropped the last shovel-full of rubbish into the bin.

'Five shillings.' Vincent replied.

'Not bad.' Barton surveyed the floor. 'And with practice your sweeping might come up to scratch.' He rubbed his chin with his forefinger. 'Right then, see you at eight o'clock on Saturday, you're on trial. I'll pay you three shillings, finish at four and bring your own dinner.'

Convinced that the dank smell of soil and old vegetables lingered on his school clothes, Vincent waited on a windy corner for a while wafting his coat open wide and planning how he would spend his three shillings. He knew his mother wouldn't be impressed by a job on a market stall; she might even try to stop him going back. He'd tell her he was helping out in an office - that would keep her quiet. Barton's Quality Produce might not be his first choice of a workplace, but at least he would have some decent money - he might even pack up his newspaper round.

'Oh no,' he thought, 'the evening papers.' He ran to the newsagent's planning how we would soft soap Mr Blackledge with some tale about a teacher keeping him late at school.

* * *

That first Saturday Vincent got up before his parents. He didn't want Sheila or John to see him setting off for work. He wriggled the too-short blue trousers down towards his hips and stretched his jumper past his waist. It was one he'd hidden under his bed, refusing to wear it ever since his mother had darned the elbows. The brown Fair Isle clashed with the trousers but he had no choice. Stuffing the packet of sandwiches his mother had made into his already bulging bag, he crept out of the house.

Barton encouraged a brisk trade with his knock-down prices and he kept Vincent busy sweeping the floor, making trips to the lock-up to replenish the stall and weighing bags of potatoes, carrots, cabbage and swede. Forced rhubarb was plentiful and Barton pointed out that every allotment owner in the town was his best pal - their left overs were enough to supply a battalion. It didn't matter that the other stalls had already had their pick of the best fruit and veg', Barton's prices were the lowest.

Rinsing the fruit and vegetables under the standpipe behind the market square had taken almost half an hour. Barton had reckoned it would take ten minutes. He'd probably go mad but what did he expect – sixty or seventy stalls sharing two water taps? Oranges with clouds of mould yielded to fingers; carrots softened with age; apples were bashed and dented. Everything that Barton bought was verging on putrefaction.

Vincent reached into the bottom of the sack. The potatoes were rotten and slimy between his fingers and the stench scoured the lining of his nose. The paper sack gave way splattering stinking mush onto the floor, splashing his shoes. He scraped the mess on to scraps of cardboard and dumped it in the bin. He'd recovered more than half of the fruit, but a haul of twelve small potatoes from almost quarter of a sack was a poor harvest.

He turned off the tap, spread out the last batch of saleable produce, patted it dry with his tea towel and loaded up his cart. He checked all around and, pulling his cap down over his forehead, he set off back to the greengrocer. Vincent's progress was slow, it was late morning and browsers packed the narrow passageways between the canvas-topped stalls scrutinising each display as though they were judges at a county show.

When he reached Barton's stall, Vincent unloaded his cart; he had a dozen boxes and placed them into three piles, more careful now that his boss was watching.

'Is that it?' Barton rested his hands on the overspill of his hips, his khaki overall straining between the three middle buttons. 'Put the cart away lad, someone will trip over it there.' He inspected the boxes, shaking his head. 'I've shown you how to sort the good from the bad. I hope you haven't been chucking away any decent stuff, I'll have it out of your wages.'

'No, Mr Barton, most of it was rotten. I've rinsed and dried the ones I could save. This is everything that we could put on the stall.'

'Well you'll have to do better. I can't make a living if you throw away half my stock.' He took off his glasses and rubbed the lenses with a screwed-up handkerchief. 'See those leaves?' Using his glasses, he gestured towards a couple of boxes under the stall. 'Get them wrapped in newspaper, about a pound in each one, they'll go for rabbit food,' Barton turned away muttering. 'Not that my customers' rabbits will ever see them.'

Vincent dragged out one of the boxes, grabbed a handful of leaves and dropped them into the brass weighing pan. Watching the scales, he added a few more to move the pointer past the pound mark and then wrapped the leaves in a sheet of newspaper. Barton's voice rose above the background chitchat of the other stallholders.

'Picture of health you are Mrs Charnock, have you been away? Yes, I've put two pounds of new potatoes in your bag, tastier than Jersey Royals they are. I've kept them especially for you. See you next week – thanks very much. Now ladies, who's next?'

Vincent could almost hear Barton's smile - the switch between grumbling and fawning was instant, frequent and unpredictable. He was fairly sure that the potatoes Barton had just sold were small rather than new. By mid-afternoon only overpriced and inessential goods remained on sale, yet people insisted on making the Saturday afternoon pilgrimage to the market and the alleyways were still packed. As his mother had said, coat billowing as she rushed out of the house a few weeks ago, 'There might be a glut and we don't want to miss out.'

It was ten past five when Vincent picked up the last cardboard box of rubbish and took it to the oversized bins behind the back wall of the market. Before he had chance to throw the box into a bin, an old man stinking of urine grabbed it, delving into the waste as though he had lost something valuable. Vincent stepped backwards letting go of the box. The man coughed and spat, his phlegm mixing into the sludge that surrounded him. Vincent screwed up his face and left.

Barton was waiting for him at the empty stall.

'You've not done too bad for a first day. Here you are, and don't spend it all at once. See you next Saturday, on time.'

Vincent picked up his canvas bag from under the stall, checked the coins and dropped them into the inside pocket of the bag. He ran off across the market square and, taking the back streets, headed for home jumping puddles as he went.

Almost home and still hurrying, he approached Audley Bridge and nipped down the steep narrow path that led from the road to the canal. Under the bridge, where no one could see him, he slipped off his shirt and trousers, took his smart clothes out of his duffle bag and put them on. Market dust covered his shoes and he picked some dock leaves to wipe them. He folded his market clothes, rammed them into the bag, climbed back up the path and, thinking about what he would buy with his wages, strolled the rest of the way home.

Sheila asked him all about his job. It wasn't difficult to convince his mother that he was working for his teacher's friend. Vincent made up a story about helping with invoices and sorting papers into alphabetical order knowing that she had no idea about office work. He pictured the man who collected the rent on Friday evenings as he described his new boss - black moustache, pasty-looking, wearing a baggy suit.

It was lucky that he'd queued with Sheila to collect her divi' from the co-op last month. He'd peered into the office and watched the two women typing surrounded by shelves stacked with papers and files. Vincent explained the layout of his invented workplace, happy to make his mother smile, reinforcing her vision of his future. It was only a white lie - he meant no harm to anybody.

It was on his second week working for Barton, on one of his errands to the lock-up, that he heard Alice's voice coming from behind.

'Vincent?'

He turned around.

'What are you doing here? I thought...'

'I'll explain later, just don't say anything, please. I'll call for you about seven, we can go to a cafe in town.' He continued on to the lock-up but as he looked back between the shoppers he could see that Alice hadn't moved. She was wearing her new mac', belted tight around her waist. Her hair, shining under the glow of market stall lights, contrasted with the headscarves on the women that surrounded her. Her mouth was open slightly.

Inside the lock-up he lifted a sack of onions above his head and slammed it down on a tray of tomatoes. Juice squirted over his trousers.

Disarmed

It's such a shocking sight first time inside
The big house for
Bad lads. There's no escape, no place to hide
Bars on every window and an exit door
Bolted until the end of each sentence.
Lock 'em up, forget 'em, the tabloids cry
The men that do wrong should be put away
And those filthy cells can be their penance.
Our lust for revenge we shall satisfy -
Seven months is our price and you must pay.

Three men armed with regimental tattoos
Wear old tracksuits,
A sad replacement for their greys and blues
Once proper soldiers, in line, shiny boots.
We sent them on crusades, smart, proud and brave

But on return dumped them without a home
Or job - no wonder they end up in jail.
Is this how we repay the youth they gave?
Desert our boys, their actions disown
We're experts in blame when our heroes fail.

One man exchanges past guns for new books,
Reading support
Twice each week might keep him from career crooks
For whom bullying is just a blood sport.
It's a brave new world, at least for an hour,
Where people and places are much better.
His skills improve and the stories inspire
Him to write and use this new found power.
To the tabloids he fires one brief letter:
Help the soldiers you no longer require.

Exodus

People treading across our TV screens,
Seeking safety from an uncivil war,
Invade our havens with their cries and screams
Caused by torments they can withstand no more.
Multitudes washed-up on Europe's strange shore
Cram onto old coaches that sag with hope
To search for a promised land like tribes before;
Pushed on by governments unable to cope.
Leaders and bishops and drinkers in bars
Discuss the news while winter advances
Fast. Unseen wounds will leave visible scars
As the seas swell and a boat capsizes.
I watch a new channel, something funny
My conscience is clear - I've sent some money.

A.J. Walker

What I write

My mind is driven by flash prompts on the web, where quirky photographs or simple phrases lead me to create one off pieces of throw away pap or sideways genius; the latter all too infrequently. I'm always surprised at where the pieces, even the shortest ones, end up. I'm getting to a critical point now. A crossroads, where the sign posts are varied 'Screenplay', 'Novella', 'Poetry', 'Novel'. I'm undecided but I'm going to take another road. The flash world has been fun, and I won't leave it entirely, but a new challenge awaits and I won't be using a map.

Christmas: Plausible Deniability

Explosive devices and a class of five year olds would have created less of a mess in her kitchen than Sue had.

She stood in the centre of the blast zone, pulling her hair, trying to recall why she'd volunteered to have Christmas at their house.

The phone rang three times - the signal that David had picked up his mum and was on his way.

She could hardly imagine her mother-in-law's reaction when she saw came in to see the kitchen chaos - Dick Cheney could take top tips from her interrogation and torture techniques. Sue cried trying to imagine an excuse - with plausible deniability - for such epic disorder.

The Chase

The man chasing me down was huge, fit and younger. It was going to take guile and luck to escape.

I darted down the alley beside the chip shop if he wasn't familiar with the area I had a chance. A broken pallet gave me a start over a fence and after unsnagging myself I was in the garden of the Drunken Duck. On the other side of the beer garden I found the gate latch jammed hard. 'Bugger!'

Minutes later, the rusty latch and soggy timber splinters lay on the floor. My hands holding a brick were filthy and scarred, my Sunday trousers torn and covered in slime.

Down the alley I saw him pristine, like he'd not broken sweat. He filled the alley like a butcher's dog. I was done for.

As his hand came out, his high pitch voice surprised me. 'Excuse me, mate, you dropped your wallet.'

The Special One

I kind of admired Colin sometimes. But mostly I was jealous. All the attention was on him. I was ignored. The older brother could look after himself. I heard them say that.

Then I saw a programme about kids with head problems. They seemed normal to me. Special kids they said. I was special. Though no one knew.

I came up with the idea by myself. Because I'm special.

I drew a paper boy. Not one that delivers papers. Just a boy on paper.

I used Colin's crayons. I made the shoes red like Colin's favourite trainers. I wanted some like that but Dad wouldn't get me them. Anyway, I drew my paper boy like a scary adult but as a boy with a big fat head. I put a scar on his fat head and didn't draw any hair. Like my dad when he was young. He used to be a skinny head. I don't know how his head could have been smaller though. That's weird.

Anyway, I drew a skinny head boy with a scar, red trainers and razor teeth. For tearing live animals into bits. And maybe even parents too. They were brilliant.

And I drew skulls on the T-shirt. Except they weren't really on the T-shirt, they were in Colin's belly. Did I say it was Colin? Anyway, it was. And he'd eaten young babies and their pets and you could see the bones through his X-ray T-shirt.

Then the clever part was I put the picture under his bed. And then Mum found it. My parents were worried. They talked quietly for days about it.

Then they talked to Colin. He said it wasn't his. That he didn't know how it had got under his bed.

Then he got treated differently. He went quieter. Special doctors came to talk to him. Then some social people. I don't know what that meant. But he was taken away so they must have bought him from Mum and Dad.

They go and visit him sometimes. I won't go.

I'm the special one again. Dad bought me red trainers.

One day I'll get razor teeth.

The Butterfly Effect

Beauty and wonder surrounds me, I am turned each day by its colour and surprises. The carpet of grass this morning was kissed softly by dew. As the sun rose it was reflected a million times in these miniature glass beads. A million times I am blessed.

The ponderous bees bob and weave through the lavender despite their mathematic probability. How can a bee fly? I have honey with my toast in celebration and thanks to their industry. Cheers, bees!

The coffee hit stirs me and my eyes are spiked by the flickering patterns of butterflies in the long grass. Their beauty is otherworldly. They appear painted by children, designed by innocence. I am dumbfounded.

I am thinking beneath a cloudless blue sky. Blue sky thinking. There is not a word to do justice to this moment. I am in a place beyond belief.

Take the time to look and think. Crack open a jar of honey. Smell the coffee and listen to the birds. Watch the flowers unfurl and their painted visitors. For you are here, too.

Under the Lowering Sun

Philip walked across the beach below the flotsam and jetsam line feeling each footfall sink into the wet sand, like through fresh snow without the crunch. He mused that - but for the large bag he was carrying - anyone seeing him in his suit and Dr Marten's would have wondered whether he was to re-enact Reggie Perrin.

The old lighthouse at the end of the spit, as always, evoked memories of his childhood trips. It had been popular with families back then, but since the lighthouse became unmanned the undulating road through the dunes had became more holes than tarmac and now only the coastguard came out here for their periodic maintenance.

It had been five years since Philip had used this beach; time enough. He felt the dead weight of the bag and shifted it, releasing the burn across his palm, as he continued towards the lighthouse.

The tide was turning and the ocean had come to an eerie stop as if someone had pressed pause. He felt time was reflecting whether to restart the seas.

Eventually ripples then small waves began lapping up the beach. He watched them to be sure the tide had turned, like he had as a child, seeing them get ever further; he wasn't sure why he found it uplifting. He realised he'd stopped walking, mesmorised by the planet's twice daily battle with the moon. Whilst there wasn't going to be anyone around there was no sense in this nostalgic dawdling.

The gulls, which had been on mute, restarted their garish calls as they turned in towards the land - seemingly led by the water's edge. They wheeled around, pink under the lowering sun, sometimes appearing as if they were hovering as they faced into the wind.

Philip judged he'd walked far enough, gratefully placing the bag down which spread like a dropped ice cream across the sand. He wasted no time opening it, then began the task of disposing the remaining body parts, throwing them along the beach as if sowing a field. Within a few days the meaty morsels would be spread miles along the coast; degrading, unrecognisable.

The gulls proved hungry too.

My Truth, Invisible

Sometimes I'm not sure whether our Adjuni magic is real or an illusion – or hallucination. Whether we are bolstered by our belief. Or whether our enemy's fear is based on theirs.

I'd always been taught that as I was not of strength or agile that I would need something to help me do what I do best; not be noticed. My options were limited. The obvious one had to be the hardest task (not requiring strength); the retrieval of our totem from the Canuchi; five years had passed since they'd stolen it. Our heart had been stolen by this act. We were diminished. Emasculated. They were too many and strong. Armed with their wands of fire and magic.

Shamen told me: I would need stealth; invisibility. As instructed, I caught and kept a flying fox for 28 days. I was to drink then of its blood: to gain invisibility for a day (time enough to get to the current Canuchi settlement). To sweep in and out. Unseen. With our totem. My adulthood our tribe's pride bought for the price of a bat's life.

I knew ten days in that I would never kill it. I fed it. Looked into its bulging eyes. Laughed at its silly tongue. At its weak attempts to escape. It lived through me. Because of me. How could I now kill it? Drink its blood from its wrung out body?

On my day of age I left the village. Cloaked only in my own belief. And hope.

I was lucky. They'd been celebrating one of their own. Four days had left much of their settlement in sleep or suffering hallucinations. I walked straight through. If people saw me they didn't believe their eyes. I was invisible.

Back home I became our king for a day; then a week. They thought I'd taken the blood. I didn't tell them. They didn't need to know I doubted the magic. I released my bat one night. I'd like to think it flies around me from time to time, but suspect the worst.

To my village, with our totem back, I am now (and will remain) the Batman.

The Moon or Chelsea

"I know what they say about me - 'you can't buy class' well I can. I can buy the class, the school, the whole bloody education system.

Don't look at me like that. I know that's not what they mean by class, I'm not completely stupid

The point is I'm super rich. Richer than most countries. Yet people look down on me. I'm not apologising for having the cahones and the luck when opportunity knocked.

Hey, look at the moon. I could get you there. Just give me a kiss and it's yours. No?

How about I bring it down to you piece by piece and rebuild it on earth for you? Everyone likes a rockery.

No, better still; I know. I'll take it apart and put it back together in my image. The moon an image of me looking down on everyone. Irony, yes?

Ha! That, my friend, is class."

Lessons in Love

Elizabeth sighed deeper than a Yorkshire gully. "Oh, Mother! What shall become of me? I thought Percy was the one."

She dabbed her nose. She'd a good feel for what forlorn should look like.

Esme looked to the ceiling and, although it wasn't for the first time that day, she saw a cobweb. She was mortified - someone in the cleaning staff would be getting a tender lessoning later. But first things first: her remaining free daughter.

"Whatever gave you that idea, my dear Elizabeth?" she said.

Elizabeth looked up from her kerchief. "Well, he told me he was the one. I believed him, too."

"Oh dear child, have you listened to anything I've told you?" Esme said.

Elizabeth shrugged, forcing out a stifled sob.

"Well, love - it was love. What do you know of love, Mother?"

It was Esme's time to sigh.

"What I meant was in these modern times. Clearly, I know you love papa deeply," Elizabeth said.

The door opened and Alice came in with tea. Esme scrutinised her, wondering when she'd last been on cleaning duty. After the tea had been put down on the afternoon table Esme returned to the conversation.

"Love, Elizabeth, is neither here nor there. It is time you realised that and take yourself a man with means. Any man. Love can come later," said Esme. "If necessary."

Super Sunday

Sundays always used to be
        dark and dreary in memory.
Black and white movies on TV,
        giant roasts, as big as me
Now grown up,
        well, nearly,
it's still spent with the TV

Super Sunday footy heaven,
in the pub until eleven
with a pint, or maybe seven,
        kebab later,
        well that's a given.
Footy's on, so get a bev in,
check out the girl who is servin'.
Sunday's for football, not for church,
no need to leave me in the lurch
if you want to do some praying
footy's what to put your faith in.

Glyn Williams

What I write

I write what I am: an Anglo-Celt in his mid-60s; semi-retired; male, white and middle-class. I write fiction and non-fiction. In publishing terms, the latter (mostly about football or opera) is reasonably successful. Not so the fiction. I have completed four novels and scores of short stories, all of them stored away. 'Proper' poetry is reserved for the woman I love. Song lyrics, on the other hand, come easier and are usually accompanied by my music. I also pen dramas, ranging from short sketches for specific occasions to full length plays and operas. Forget publication – some of them have been *performed*!

Four Songs About Something

1. Eskimos

I'm an Eskimo called Joe,
And I spend my time just wishin'
I don't have to go out fishin'
Through the ice.
It isn't nice!

My wife's an Eskimo called Flo,
And the thing she wants to stop
Is eating blubber till we drop.
It's bad, she thinks,
Tastes vile and stinks!

For we have a dream that pretty soon we should
Have a proper house that's made of bricks or stone or wood.
A dwelling that won't melt when winter's through,
With a kitchen and a big loo
Instead of that foul igloo!

My kid's an Eskimo called Mo.
She'd like some toys that aren't as real
As local polar bear and seal!
They're cold and smelly.
She wants a telly!

For we have a dream that fairly soon we might
Have a condo with Jacuzzi and some warmth and light!
A house not built of snow by my own hand,
With an oven and a pan, dear,
Perhaps a plot of land, dear?

We are Eskimos, we know,
The Arctic Circle is our home,

Across its frozen wastes we roam.
We'd like a chance
To live in France!
Or maybe heaven's
A house in Devon!
Perhaps we'd rule
In Liverpool!

2. Maths

Let's do the algorithm rhythm!
But no more sex in the googolplex!
Let's show a 'Go!' sign to the cosine.
Let's really try to take a slice of pi!
Spelt 'P-I'!

Let's aim to find a plangent tangent!
But, please, no rhombus in the rumpus room!
With a nice equilateral triangle
We can be acute from every single angle!
Fangle-dangle!

Middle section 1
Those isosceles and vertices,
They sound like some absurd disease.
Trapezia and calculus and matrix
Will only lead to levity and play tricks
On all those Asians
Who like equations!

Let's do the algorithm rhythm!
But no more sex in the googolplex!
Let's show a 'Go!' sign to the cosine.
Let's really try to take a slice of pi!
Spelt 'P-I'!

Middle section 2
The Riemann zeta function
Will take us to the junction
Where decagons and segments often meet.
Oh, what a treat!
They're square but neat!

Let's do the algorithm rhythm!
But just one vector and please don't hector!
If Fibonacci seems so starchy,
Let's try to relax with numbers prime!
And take our time!

Let's do the algorithm rhythm!
But no more sex in the googolplex!
Let's show a 'Go!' sign to the cosine.
Let's really try to take a slice of pi!
Spelt 'P-I'!
Yes, spelt 'P-I'!

Coda
But there's bad news!
I've got those Chinese Postman Theorem Blues?
Oh, yeah!

3. Endangered species

Chorus 1
Whatever happened to my friend the Dinosaur?
Whatever happened to the Dodo?
You can't find a Woolly Mammoth when you need one!
And the Buffalo's the next one that may go!

Verse 1
There are creatures great and small, we all agree,
Who lead happy lives and roam the planet free.

But there are others from their manger
Who exist in mortal danger.
They are facing the distinction
Of a terrible extinction!

Chorus 2
Whatever happened to my friend the Yukon Horse?
What happened to the Mastodon?
Yes, the Bowhead and the Muskox seemed contented:
One minute they were there, the next one gone!

Verse 2
The Siberian Tiger's almost disappeared!
There are fewer Armadillos than we feared!
While the beautiful Snow Leopard, he
Is facing total jeopardy!
And Giant Panda and Blue Whale
Are species that may fail!

Chorus 3
Whatever happened to Tyrannosaurus Rex?
Whatever happened to the Dhole?
Did Panoplosaurus Minus die of boredom
Or fall into a deep and dismal hole?

Verse 3
There are Polar Bears and Rhinos on the list.
There's the Albatross and Turtle – they'll be missed!
There's the Wolverine and Manatee
(Whatever they may be)
And there are Wild Dogs and Hyenas
That we soon may never see!

Chorus 4
Whatever happened to my friend the Dinosaur?
Whatever happened to the Dodo?

You can't find a Woolly Mammoth when you need one!
And the Buffalo's the next one that may go!
Yes, the Buffalo's the next one that may go!

4. Global warming (waltz)

1. On a hot beach in Iceland we lay,
'Cos the ice-caps had melted away.
Now Iceland's a nice land
With palm trees not geysers,
With fun-fairs and bandstands
And Bacardi Breezers!
The oceans and rivers were rising,
Lots of creatures were drowned, not surprising!
The greenhouse effect was in force
And poor Africa deluged, of course!

2. On the tropical Island of Skye,
Where the hot steaming jungle grows high,
Now Scotland's a hot land
With deserts not mountains
Beach parties and surfing
And sweet champagne fountains!
The glens and the castles are hidden
And the kilt and the whisky forbidden!
The greenhouse effect is in force
And poor England has vanished, of course!

Countermelody
3. Global warming, so alarming!
Hot and arid, not so charming!
Greenhouse madness, global sadness!
Greenhouse gases, kick their asses!

4. On the ocean of Europe we sailed,
Our defence of the planet had failed.

For London is gone
And St Petersburg's hist'ry,
The reason, my good friend,
Is surely no myst'ry.
St Paul's is now coated in shellfish
All because we were stupid and selfish,
The greenhouse effect is in force
And St Helens has sunken, of course.
And St Helens has sunken, of course.

Verses 1 and 3 should now be sung together, numbers allowing.

The Journey

Imagine a journey. Not just a stroll to the next village or an afternoon bus ride to visit a favourite aunt or cousin on the other side of the county. Not even a long train or bus journey from one end of the country to the other. This is a mighty long journey that may take many months to complete. Perhaps years. Your starting point is the fertile hillside where the vines grow tall and where you live happily but alone. Your destination is a mighty citadel. Looking southwest from your hillside, you can see it in the distance, across mountains and valleys. In the day its towers and golden domes glint in the sunlight. In the evening its streetlights twinkle in the dark. You have heard of it as a magical and wondrous place and something deep inside compels you to visit it.

You set off on foot alone. The weather is good, with the morning sun shining from behind your left shoulder. The road slopes gently downwards and progress is easy. You pass through hamlets and small townships. Some people smile and say hello. Others ignore you. You stop for food and drink, later to sleep. Someone asks you who you are and what you are doing. You would rather not tell them about your journey to the citadel – not yet – but you are persuaded. Some respond with mild interest but most with indifference.

The weather changes. The temperature drops, dark clouds glower and you feel rain on your face. Now the road swings steeply upwards. There are few settlements in this part of the country so you spend long, dark nights sheltering in cold and otherwise deserted log cabins. The only sign of human life is the occasional traveller heading in the opposite direction. You try to strike up a conversation but the traveller is also struggling against the hostile elements and moves on without comment. After many days – perhaps weeks – the air warms and the road begins to fall. The sunlight that flooded your hillside returns and in the distance you catch sight of your goal: the citadel, shimmering in the dusk. You study the terrain. A few more hills to climb and valleys to cross and you will almost be there. You regain your spirit and a spring returns to your step. The citadel disappears from view as you clamber up another hill. You hear the sound of rushing water and see at the foot of this hill, far below, something you did not expect: a mighty river.

The river is wide and deep, its foaming current flowing strongly westwards to your right. Like Orpheus on the bank of the Styx, anxious to cross over to Hades and his beloved Eurydice, you seek a ferryman: a skilled mariner who can pilot you across in safety. Other travellers gather at the riverside. You notice a fat sailor and ask him to take you across. He seems jolly at first but his expression is soured by thin lips and a sly look in his eyes. You cannot determine if he is a man or a woman. He behaves like a man but not the sort of man you would choose as a friend. He asks about your journey and you tell him about the citadel. He smiles wryly. 'I haven't been there myself and wouldn't recommend it. It's not for the likes of you.' 'But you would take me across if I paid you the right fare?' He looks first at you and then at a small group of figures huddled by a boat some distance downstream. 'My crew and a band of travellers bound for an island out at sea. I can't help you.' You notice another pilot, a tall, handsome woman with kind eyes. She agrees to take you across and the two of you select a willing crew. After many days preparing your boat for the journey, you finally set sail and steer a course across the mighty waterway. The river is calm at first but less than halfway across the wind picks up, the boat starts to toss and progress is halted. The boat hits a rock and two of the oarsmen plunge overboard. The pilot's fellow sailors reach out desperately and hoist one to safety. The other is swept away. It is no good. The little boat is too badly damaged to continue the journey. The tiller is turned and you allow the current to sweep you back to shore. The fat ferryman's crew and passengers are still huddled by his boat but there is no sign of him. He has disappeared, lured away by rich rewards on another river.

You remain by the shore, living in a mean guesthouse, for many months. No-one comes and no-one goes. The fat ferryman's crew and passengers disperse and the tall, handsome ferrywoman can be seen plying her trade along the near shore. You are beginning to despair of ever crossing the mighty river, of ever seeing the citadel. Winter and spring pass and the waters calm. Someone tells you that the fat ferryman has been replaced by an unknown pilot with little experience but good manners and a pleasing demeanour. He is on his way to the village but currently staying with his uncle in a nearby village. You send him a scribbled note introducing yourself and telling him about the citadel. Two weeks elapse. A young man with straw-coloured hair and a soft boyish face knocks on your door. He introduces himself. 'I have a crew,' he says. 'We can sail tomorrow.' He tells you that there are other people who want to cross over. He suggests we meet them. He will take only people you approve of. The following morning you meet him by the fat ferryman's old boat. There is a crew of four strong oarsmen and a small group wanting to join you as passengers. You tell them about your journey and the citadel. They smile and nod to each other. You are so pleased by their interest that you allow them all to join you. With a fair wind, the four strong oarsmen and the skilful piloting of the young ferryman, you soon cross the river and disembark on a welcoming sandy beach. You thank the ferryman and his crew and bid farewell to your fellow travellers. You begin to walk away from the shore. 'You do not understand,' the young ferryman shouts after you. 'We do not want merely to cross the river with you. We want to accompany you to the citadel. You have described it as a magical and wondrous place, but are its magic and wonder for you alone?' You tell them the citadel is for whoever is willing to make the journey. You have misjudged the difficulties of this journey. There are many more hills to climb, valleys to cross and streams to ford, but the young ferryman tells you he has maps to find the way. As you pass through further hamlets and villages you and your fellow travellers tell other people about your journey. Few on this side of the mighty river, though they are closer than the people who crossed with you, have seen the citadel. But their interest is aroused. Some join you, bringing food, drink, songs and renewed enthusiasm to your progress. You rest overnight in an inn less than a day away from your destination. As you sit in the humble refectory eating a simple meal with the others you realise this is no longer your journey. It is a journey shared with enthusiasm by all the people with you. Without your fellow passengers to sustain and support you, without your strong oarsmen to take you across the mighty river and, above all, without the guidance on sea and land of the young ferryman, you would not be here.

The following morning you climb one last hill. As you reach the summit the citadel suddenly appears in view. It is just a few yards away. Its walls and towers are painted white and its golden domes sparkle brilliantly in the morning sun. You follow your fellow passengers through the citadel's broad oak gates. The cobbled street is lined with cheering crowds. Some join you. Your way is strewn with flowers. Men shake your hand and women and children kiss you. The citadel's young mayor steps forward and applauds your company as it passes. He takes you to one side. 'Welcome! This journey has been made by many people, but once upon a time it existed only in your imagination, I think.' You nod. 'Yes, but when it was just in my imagination it did not really exist. I dreamt it, but other people have made it real.'

The journey home is surprisingly quick and uneventful. A few weeks later you find yourself sitting once more on your fertile hillside where the vines grow tall. You look across to the citadel. You hope one day to visit it again. You look in other directions. Perhaps there are citadels elsewhere you might like to visit.